BRITISH COMMITTEES, COMMISSIONS, AND COUNCILS OF TRADE AND PLANTATIONS, 1622–1675

LECTOR HOUSE PUBLIC DOMAIN WORKS

BRITISH COMMITTEES, COMMISSIONS, AND COUNCILS OF TRADE AND PLANTATIONS, 1622–1675

CHARLES MCLEAN ANDREWS

ISBN: 978-93-5614-017-2

Published: 1908

LECTOR HOUSE LLP

LECTOR HOUSE LLP
E-MAIL: lectorpublishing@gmail.com

Series XXVI   Nos. 1–2–3

JOHNS HOPKINS UNIVERSITY STUDIES
IN
HISTORICAL AND POLITICAL SCIENCE

Under the Direction of the
Departments of History, Political Economy, and Political Science

BRITISH COMMITTEES, COMMISSIONS, AND COUNCILS OF TRADE AND PLANTATIONS, 1622–1675

BY

CHARLES M. ANDREWS

Professor of History

1908

CONTENTS

APPENDIX

BRITISH COMMITTEES, COMMISSIONS, AND COUNCILS OF TRADE AND PLANTATIONS, 1622–1675.

CHAPTER I.

CONTROL OF TRADE AND PLANTATIONS UNDER JAMES I AND CHARLES I.

In considering the subject which forms the chief topic of this paper, we are not primarily concerned with the question of settlement, intimately related though it be to the larger problem of colonial control. We are interested rather in the early history of the various commissions, councils, committees, and boards appointed at one time or another in the middle of the seventeenth century for the supervision and management of trade, domestic, foreign, and colonial, and for the general oversight of the colonies whose increase was furthered, particularly after 1650, in largest part for commercial purposes. The coupling of the terms "trade" and "foreign plantations" was due to the prevailing economic theory which viewed the colonies not so much as markets for British exports or as territories for the receipt of a surplus British population—for Great Britain had at that time no surplus population and manufactured but few commodities for export—but rather as sources of such raw materials as could not be produced at home, and of such tropical products as could not be obtained otherwise than from the East and West Indies. The two interests were not, however, finally consolidated in the hands of a single board until 1672, after which date they were not separated until the final abolition of the old Board of Trade in 1782. It is, therefore, to the period before 1675 that we shall chiefly direct our attention, in the hope of throwing some light upon a phase of British colonial control that has hitherto remained somewhat obscure. Familiar as are many of the facts connected with the early history of Great Britain's management of trade and the colonies, it is nevertheless true that no attempt has been made to trace in detail the various experiments undertaken by the authorities in England in the interest of trade and the plantations during the years before 1675. Many of the details are, and will always remain, unknown, nevertheless it is possible to make some additions to our knowledge of a subject which is more or less intimately related to our early colonial history.

Before 1622, Privy Council the sole authority

At the beginning of colonization the control of all matters relating to trade and the plantations lay in the hands of the king and his council, forming the executive branch of the government. Parliament had not yet begun to legislate for the colonies, and in matters of trade and commerce the parliaments of James I accomplished much less than had those of Elizabeth. "In the time of James I," says Dr. Prothero, "it was more essential to assert constitutional principles and to maintain parliamentary rights than to pass new laws or to create new institutions." Thus the Privy Council became the controlling factor in all matters that concerned the colonies and it acted in the main without reference or delegation to others, since the practice of appointing advisory boards or deliberative committees, though not unknown, was at first employed only as an occasional expedient. The councils of James I were called upon to deal with a wide variety of colonial business—letters, petitions, complaints and reports from private individuals, such as merchants, captains of ships voyaging to the colonies, seamen, prisoners, and the like, from officials in England, merchant companies, church organizations, and colonial governments, notably the governor and council and assembly of Virginia. To all these communications the Council replied either by issuing orders which were always mandatory, or by sending letters which often contained information and advice as well as instructions. It dealt with the Virginia Company in London and sent letters, both before and after the dissolution of the company, to the governor and council in Virginia, and in all these letters trade played an important part. For example, the order of October 24, 1621, which forbade the colony to export tobacco and other commodities to foreign countries, declared that such a privilege as an open trade on the part of the colony was desirable "neither in policy nor for the honor of the state (that being but a colony derived from hence)," and that it could not be suffered "for that it may be a loss unto his Majesty in his customs, if not the hazarding of the trade which in future times is well hoped may be of much profit, use, and importance to the Commonalty."[1] Similarly the Council issued a license to Lord Baltimore to export provisions for the relief of his colony at Avalon,[2] ordered that the *Ark* and the *Dove*, containing Calvert and the settlers of Maryland, be held back at Tilbury until the oaths of allegiance had been taken,[3] and instructed the governor and company of Virginia to give friendly assistance to Baltimore's undertaking.[4]

Commission of Trade, 1622–1623

Of the employment of committees or special commissions to inquire into questions either commercial or colonial there is no evidence before the year 1622. A few months after the dissolution of the third Stuart parliament, James I issued a proclamation for the encouragement of trade, and directed a special commission not composed of privy councillors to inquire into the decay of the clothing trade and to report to the Privy Council such remedial measures as seemed best adapted

---

[1] Privy Council Register, James I, Vol. V, p. 173; repeated p. 618.
[2] P.C.R., Charles I. Vol. V, p. 106.
[3] P.C.R., Charles I, Vol. IX, p. 291.
[4] Cal. State Papers, Colonial, 1574–1660, p. 170, § 78.

to increase the wealth and prosperity of the realm.[5] At the same time he caused a commission to be issued to the Lord Keeper, the Lord Treasurer, the Lord President of the Council and others "to collect and cause a true survey to be taken in writing of the names, qualities, professions, and places of habitation of such strangers as do reside within the realm of England and use any retailing trade or handicraft trade and do reform the abuses therein according to the statutes now in force."[6] The commissioners of trade duly met, during the years 1622 and 1623, summoned persons to appear before them, and reported to the Council. Their report was afterward presented to the King sitting with the Council at Wansted, "was allowed and approved of, and commandment was given to enter it in the Register of Counsell causes and to remain as an act of Counsell by order of the Lord President."[7] There is evidence also to show that the commission issued orders on its own account, for in June, 1623, the Mayor and Aldermen of the city of London wrote two letters to the commission expressing their approval of its orders and sending petitions presented to them by citizens of London.[8]

Commission of Trade, 1625–1626

On April 15, 1625, less than three weeks after the death of James I, a warrant was issued by his successor for a commission of trade, the duties of which were of broader and more general character than were those of the previous body.[9] The first record of its meeting is dated January 18, 1626, but it is probable that then the commission had been for some time in existence, though the exact date when its commission was issued is not known. The text of both commission and instructions are among the Domestic Papers.[10] The board was to advance the exportations of home manufactures and to repress the "ungainful importation of foreign commodities." Looked upon as a subcommittee of the Privy Council, but having none of the privy councillors among its members, it was required to sit every week and to consider all questions that might be referred to it for examination and report. The fact that a complaint against the patent of Sir Ferdinando Gorges was referred to it shows that it was qualified to deal not only with questions of trade but also with plantation affairs.[11] At about the same time a committee of the Council was appointed to take into consideration a special question of trade and to make report to the Council. Neither of these bodies appears to have had more than a temporary existence, although the commission sat for some time and accomplished no inconsiderable amount of work.

Privy Council Committee of Trade, 1630–1640

The first Privy Council committee of trade that had any claim to permanency was that appointed in March, 1630, consisting at first of thirteen members, the

---

[5] Rymer, Fœdera XVII. pp. 410–414.

[6] Public Record Office, Chancery, Crown Dockets, 4, p. 280, June 26, 1622.

[7] P.C.R., James I, Vol. VI, pp. 333, 365–368, July, 1624.

[8] Analytical Index to the Series of Records known as Remembrancia preserved among the Archives of the City of London, 1579–1644, p. 526.

[9] Cal. State Papers, Domestic, 1625–1649, pp. 4, 84.

[10] Cal. State Papers, Dom., 1625–1649, pp. 225, 522, §§ 19, 20, p. 495.

[11] P.C.R., Charles I, Vol. II, Pt. I, p. 68.

Lord Keeper, the Lord Treasurer, the Lord President, the Lord Privy Seal, Earl Marshall, the Lord Steward, Earl of Dorset, Earl of Holland, Earl of Carlisle, Lord Dorchester, the Vice-Chamberlain, Sir Henry Cottington and Mr. Secretary Coke. This committee was to meet on Friday mornings. The same committee, with the omission of one member, was appointed the next year to meet on Tuesdays in the afternoon. In 1634 the membership was reduced to nine, but in 1636, 1638 and 1639, by the addition of the Lord Treasurer, the number was raised to ten, as follows: the Lord President, the Lord Treasurer, the Lord Keeper, the Lord Privy Seal, Earl Marshall, Earl of Dorset, Lord Cottington, Mr. Comptroller, Mr. Secretary Coke and Mr. Secretary Windebank. The meetings were again held on Fridays, though on special occasions the committee was warned to meet on other days by order of the Council, and on one occasion at least assembled at Hampton Court.[12] To this committee were referred all matters of trade which came to the attention of the Council during the ten years, from 1630 to 1640. Notes of its meetings between 1631 and 1637 were kept by Secretaries Coke and Windebank and show the extent and variety of its activities. Except for the garbling of tobacco it does not appear to have concerned itself with plantation affairs.[13] As the King was generally present at its meetings, it possessed executive as well as advisory powers, not only making reports to the Council, but also drafting regulations and issuing orders on its own account. Occasionally it appointed special committees to examine into certain trade difficulties, and on September 21, 1638, and again on February 3, 1639, we find notice of a separate board of commissioners for trade constituted under the great seal to inquire into the decay of the clothing industry. This board sat for two years and made an elaborate report to the Privy Council on June 9, 1640.[14]

Temporary Plantation Commissions, 1630–1633

Laud Commission for Plantations, 1634–1641

Though committees for trade, ordnance, foreign affairs, and Ireland had a more or less continuous existence during the period after 1630, no similar committee for plantations was created during this decade. Temporary commissions and committees of the Council had been, however, frequently appointed. In 1623 and 1624 several sets of commissioners for Virginia were named "to inquire into the true state of Virginia and the Somers Islands plantations," "to resolve upon the well settling of the colony of Virginia," "and to advise on a fit patent for the Virginia Company." In 1631 a commission of twenty-three persons, of whom four constituted a quorum, was created, partly from within and partly from without the Privy Council, "to advise upon some course for establishing the advancement of the plantations of Virginia."[15] Similar commissions were appointed to meet

[12] P.C.R., Charles I, Vols. V, p. 10; VI, p. 7; X., p. 3; XII, p. 1; XV, p. 1.

[13] Cal. State Papers, Dom., 1629–1631, p. 526; 1634–1635, pp. 453, 472, 513, 584; 1635, pp. 30, 515, 548, 598; 1635–1636, pp. 44, 231; 1636–1637, p. 402; 1637, pp. 47; 1637–1638, p. 410. The secretaries' notes will be found as follows: Coke, 1629–1631, pp. 526, 535; Windebank, 1634–1635, pp. 500, 513; 1635, pp. 11–12, 29, 502, 536; 1635–1636, pp. 291–292, 428–429, 551–552; 1636–1637, pp. 402; 1637, p. 47.

[14] Historical MSS. Commission, Report XV. Manuscripts of the Duke of Portland, VIII, pp. 2–3.

[15] Cal. State Papers, Col., 1574–1660, pp. 44, 62, 63, 64, 130; Virginia Magazine, VIII,

special exigencies in the careers of other plantations, Somers Islands, Caribbee Islands, etc. In 1632, we meet with a committee forming the first committee of the Council appointed for the plantations, quite distinct in functions and membership from the committee for trade and somewhat broader in scope than the commissions mentioned above. The circumstances of its appointment were these: In the year 1632 complaints began to come in to the Privy Council regarding the conduct of the colony of Massachusetts Bay. Thomas Morton and Philip Ratcliffe had been banished from that colony and sent back to England. Sir Christopher Gardiner, also, after a period of troubled relations with the authorities there, had taken ship for England. These men, acting in conjunction with Gorges and Mason, whose claims had already been before the Council, presented petitions embodying their grievances. On December 19, 1632, the Council listened to the reading of these petitions and to the presentation of a "relation" drawn up by Gardiner. After long debate "upon the whole carriage of the plantation of that country," it appointed a committee of twelve members, called the Committee on the New England Plantations, with the Archbishop of York at its head, "to examine how the patents for the said plantations have been granted." This committee had power to call "to their assistance such other persons as they shall think fit," "to examine the truth of the aforesaid information or any other information as shall be presented to them and shall make report thereof to this board and of the true state of the said plantations." The committee deliberated on the "New England Case," summoned many of the "principal adventurers in that plantation" before it, listened to the complainants, and reported favorably to the colony. The essential features of its report were embodied in an order in council, dated January 19, 1633.[16] This committee, still called the Committee for New England, was reappointed in December, 1633, with a slight change of membership, Laud, who had been made primate the August before, taking the place of the Archbishop of York as chairman. But this committee was soon overshadowed by the greater commission to come.[17]

Subcommittees for Plantations, 1632–1639

The first separate commission, though, in reality, a committee of the Privy Council, appointed to concern itself with all the plantations, was created by Charles I, April 28, 1634. It was officially styled the Commission for Foreign Plantations; one petitioner called it "the Lords Commissioners for Plantations in General," and another "the learned Commissioners appointed by the King to examine and rectify all complaints from the plantations." It is probable that the term "Committee

---

pp. 29, 33–46, 149.

[16] Bradford, pp. 352–355; P.C.R., Charles I, Vol. VIII, pp. 346–347; Cal. State Papers, Col., 1574–1660, p. 158.

[17] P.C.R., Charles I, Vol. IX, p. 1. The order in Council of July 3, 1633, regarding Virginia and Lord Baltimore, is headed "Lords Commissioners for Foreign Plantations." It is evident, however, that this body is not a separate board of commissioners but the Privy Council sitting as a committee of the whole for plantations. The membership does not agree with that of the committee of 1632, that committee did not sit in the Star Chamber, and such a committee could not issue an order which the Privy Council alone could send out. There was no separate commission of this kind in July, 1633, as Tyler, England in America, pp. 122–123 (Amer. Nation Series, IV) seems to think.

of Foreign Plantations" was occasionally applied to it, as there is nothing to show that the committee of 1633 remained in existence after April, 1634.[18] Recommissioned, April 10, 1636, it continued to sit as an active body certainly as late as August, 1641, and possibly longer,[19] though there is no formal record of its discontinuance. Its original membership was as follows: William Laud, Archbishop of Canterbury; Richard Neile, Archbishop of York; Sir Thomas Coventry, the Lord Keeper; Earl of Portland, the Lord Treasurer, Earl of Manchester, the Lord Privy Seal, Earl of Arundel, the Earl Marshall, Earl of Dorset, Lord Cottington, Sir Thomas Edmondes, the Master Treasurer, Sir Henry Vane, the Master Comptroller, and the secretaries, Coke and Windebank. Later the Earl of Sterling was added.[20] Five constituted a quorum. The powers granted to the commission were extensive and almost royal in character: to make laws and orders for the government of the English colonies in foreign parts; to impose penalties and imprisonment for offenses in ecclesiastical matters; to remove governors and require an account of their government; to appoint judges and magistrates, and to establish courts, both civil and ecclesiastical; to hear and determine all manner of complaints from the colonies; to have power over all charters and patents, and to revoke those surreptitiously or unduly obtained. Such powers clearly show that the commission was designed as an instrument for enforcing the royal will in the colonies, and furnishes no precedent for the later councils and boards of trade and foreign plantations. Called into being probably because of the continued emigration of Puritans to New England, the complaints against the Massachusetts charter, and the growth of Independency in that colony, it was in origin a coercive, not an inquisitory, body, in the same class with the courts of Star Chamber and High Commission, and the Councils of Wales and the North. Unlike these bodies, it proved practically impotent, and there is nothing to show that it took any active part in the attempt to repeal the Massachusetts charter or in any important particular exercised the powers granted to it. It did not remove or appoint a governor, establish a court, or grant or revoke a charter. It received petitions either directly or from the Privy Council and made recommendations, but it never attempted to establish uniformity in New England or to bring the New England colonies more directly under the authority of the Crown. Whether it was the failure of the attempt to vacate the Massachusetts charter, or the poverty of the King, or the approach of civil war that prevented the enforcement of the royal policy, we cannot say, but the fact remains that the Laud commission played a comparatively inconspicuous part during the seven years of its existence and has gained a prominence in the history of our subject out of all proportion to its importance.

More directly connected with the commercial and colonial interests of the realm were the subcommittees which the Privy Council used during these years and earlier as advisory and inquisitory bodies. In addition to committees of its own, the Privy Council called on various outside persons known to be familiar with the circumstances of a particular case or experts in the general subject involved, and

[18] Cal. State Papers, Col., 1574–1660, pp. 184, 200, 251, 259.

[19] Cal. State Papers, Col., 1675–1676, § 193.

[20] P.C.R., Charles I, Vol. X, p. 1; XII, p. 1; XV, p. 1; Cal. State Papers, Col., 1574–1660, pp. 177, 232.

entrusted to them the consideration of important matters that had been called to its attention. As we have already seen, such a subcommittee on trade had been appointed in 1625, and after 1630 we meet with many references to individuals or groups of experts. The attorney general was called upon to examine complaints regarding New England and Maryland in 1632 and 1635; the Chancellor of London was requested to examine the parties in a controversy over a living in St. Christopher in 1637; many commercial questions were referred to special bodies of merchants or others holding official positions. In 1631 a complaint regarding interlopers in Canada was referred to a committee of three, Sir William Becher, clerk of the Council; Serj. (Wm.) Berkeley, afterward governor of Virginia, and Edward Nicholas, afterward clerk of the Council, and a new committee in which Sir William Alexander and Robert Charlton took the place of Becher and Nicholas was appointed in 1632.[21] Berkeley, Alexander, and Charlton were known as the Commissioners for the Gulf and River of Canada and parts adjacent, and were all directly interested in Canadian trade.[22] These committees received references from the Council, summoned witnesses and examined them, and made reports to the Council. Similarly, the dispute between Vassall and Kingswell was referred on March 10, 1635, to Edward Nicholas and Sir Abraham Dawes for examination and report, and because it was an intricate matter, consumed considerable time and required a second report.[23] Again a case regarding the Virginia tobacco trade was referred to the body known as the "Commissioners of Tobacco to the Lords of the Privy Council," appointed as early as 1634 and itself a subcommittee having to do with tobacco licenses, customs, and trade. The members were Lord Goring, Sir Abraham Dawes, John Jacob, and Edmund Peisley. The first specific references to "subcommittees," *eo nomine*, are of date May 23, May 25, and June 27, 1638. The last named reference mentions the receipt by the Privy Council of a "certificate" or report from Sir John Wolstenholme and Sir Abraham Dawes "unto whom their lordships had formerly referred the hearing and examining of complaints by John Michael in the Laconia case."[24] As the earlier reference of May 23 had to do with the estate of Sir Thomas Gates and that of May 25 to a Virginia matter, it is evident that this particular subcommittee had been appointed some time before May 23, 1638, and that the only thing new about it was the term "subcommittee" as applied to such a body. This conjecture seems reasonable when we note that Wolstenholme and Dawes had already served on the commission for Virginia and were thoroughly conversant with plantation affairs, while Dawes was also a member of the tobacco commission and had served on the committee in the Kingswell-Vassall case. An examination of later "subcommittees" shows that many of the same men continued to be utilized by the Council in their capacity as experts. Lord Goring, John Jacob, Sir Abraham Dawes, with Sir William Becher and Edward Nicholas, clerks of the Council, and Edward Sandys, brother of Sir Edwin Sandys, and a councillor of Virginia under Governor Wyatt, formed the subcommittee to whom, on July 15, was referred the complaint of Samuel Mathews against Governor Har-

[21] Cal. State Papers, Col., 1574–1660, pp. 9, 140, 151, 158, 211, 258.
[22] Cal. State Papers, Col., 1574–1600, p. 129.
[23] Cal. State Papers, Col., pp. 197–198, 207.
[24] P.C.R., Charles I, Vol. XV, p. 300.

vey. When the same matter was referred again to a subcommittee on October 24, Sir Dudley Carleton, formerly one of the commissioners for Virginia, and Thomas Meautys, clerk of the Council, were substituted for Dawes and Nicholas.[25] These committees were instructed "to call the parties before them, to examine the matter, and find out the truth, and then to make certificate to their lordships of the true state of things and their opinion thereof."[26] Similar references continued to be made during the year 1639, on January 4, February 22, March 8,[27] June 12, 16, July 17, 26, 28, August 28, and the evidence seems to show that the committee, though frequently changing its membership, was considered a body sitting regularly and continuously. The certificate of July 9, 1638, in answer to the reference of June 16, was signed by Sir William Becher, Thomas Meautys, Sir Francis Wyatt, and Abraham Williams; that of July 23 by Becher, Dawes, Jacob, and Williams. After August 28 we hear no more of the subcommittee. Whether this is due to a failure of the Register to enter further references and certificates or to the actual cessation of its labors, we cannot say. The committee was always appointed by the Council, and always reported to that body. Frequently its certificates are entered at length in the Register.[28] The petition upon which it acted was sometimes sent directly to itself, frequently to the Privy Council, which referred it to the subcommittee, and but rarely to the Commissioners for Foreign Plantations.[29] The committee was limited in its scope to no one colony. It reported on matters in England, New Hampshire, Massachusetts, Somers Islands, and Virginia. It dealt with secular business and ecclesiastical questions, and on one occasion at least was required to examine and approve the instructions issued to a colonial governor.[30] It does not appear ever to have acted except by order of the Privy Council, and was never in any sense of the word a subcommittee of the Commissioners of Foreign Plantations, although in reporting to the Council it was reporting to those who composed that commission.[31]

---

[25] Virginia Magazine, X, p. 428; XI, p. 46.

[26] P.C.R., Charles I, Vol. XV, p. 508.

[27] "Att Whitehall, 8th of March, 1638(9)

> Their Lordships do pray and require the subcommittee for foreign plantations to consider of this petition at their next meeting and to make report to their Lordships of their opinion concerning the same.

Will. Becher."

[28] P.C.R., Charles I, Vols. XV, p. 343; XVI, pp. 542–543.

[29] P.C.R., Charles I, Vol. XVI, p. 558; Cal. State Papers, Col., 1574–1660, p. 301.

[30] Cal. State Papers, Col., 1675–1676, § 190.

[31] The commissioners frequently formed a majority of those present at a Privy Council meeting. For example, in 1638, the Council wrote a letter to the governor of Virginia. This letter was signed by eleven councillors, of whom eight were members of the Commission. It is sometimes difficult to distinguish the different capacities in which Archbishop Laud acted. A series of minutes drawn up by him in 1638 of the subjects upon which he had prepared reports to the King notes the following: concerning the six plantations, grants of offices in reversion, new patent offices and monopolies, the execution of the King's former directions, and trade and commerce. In making these reports Archbishop Laud acted as president of the Council, president of the Commission for Foreign Plantations, president of the committee for Foreign Affairs, High Commission Court, etc.

Privy Council in control, 1640–1642

Parliamentary Commission for Plantations, 1643–1648

From 1640 to 1642 plantation business was managed by the Privy Council with the aid of occasional committees of its own appointed to consider special questions. The term "subcommittee," as we have seen, does not appear to have been used after 1639,[32] but commissions authorizing experts to make inquiry and report are referred to, and committees of the Council took into consideration questions of trade and the plantations. During the year from July 5, 1642, to June, 1643, no measures relating to the colonies appear to have been taken, for civil war was in full swing. In 1643, Parliament assumed to itself the functions of King and Council and became the executive head of the kingdom. Among the earliest acts was the appointment of a parliamentary commission of eighteen members, November 24, 1643, authorized to control plantation affairs. At its head was Robert Rich, Earl of Warwick, and among its members were Philip, Earl of Pembroke, Edward, Earl of Manchester, William, Viscount Say and Seale, Philip, Lord Wharton, and such well known Puritan commoners as Sir Arthur Haslerigg, John Pym, Sir Harry Vane, Junior, Oliver Cromwell, Samuel Vassall, and others. Four members constituted a quorum. The powers granted to this commission were extensive, though as far as phraseology goes, less complete than those granted to the commission of 1634. The commissioners were to have "power and authority to provide for, order, and dispose all things which they shall from time to time find most fit and advantageous to the well governing, securing, and strengthening, and preserving" of "all those islands and other plantations, inhabited, planted, or belonging to any of his Majesty's the King of England's subjects." They were authorized to call to their assistance any inhabitants of the plantations or owners of land in America who might be within twenty miles of their place of meeting; to make use of all records, books, and papers which concerned any of the colonies; to appoint governors and officers for governing the plantations; to remove any of the officials so appointed and to put others in their places; and, when they deemed fit, to assign as much of their authority and power to such persons as they should deem suitable for better governing and preserving of the plantations from open violence and private disturbance and destruction.

In the exercise of these powers the commissioners never embraced the full opportunity offered to them by their charter. They did appoint one governor, Sir Thomas Warner, governor of the Caribbee Islands. They granted to the inhabitants of Providence, Portsmouth, and Newport a patent of incorporation and conferred upon the patentees authority "to rule themselves by such form of civil government as by voluntary consent of all or the greater part of them they should find most suitable to their estate or condition.[33] They also endeavored to make a grant of the Narragansett country to Massachusetts, at the special request of Massachusetts' agents in 1643, but failed, partly because they had no certain authority to grant

[32] The term "subcommittee" is used by petitioners as late as August, 1640 (Cal. Col., 1574–1660, p. 314), but no references and reports of so late a date are to be found in the Calendar or the Register.

[33] This is, of course, the well-known Williams patent of 1644. Rhode Island, Colonial Records, I, pp. 143–146.

land and partly because the only clause of their commission which seemed to give such authority required the consent of a majority, and the agents could obtain but nine signatures to the grant. Even these activities on the part of the board lasted but little over a year, and after 1644 the commissioners played a more or less passive role. They continued to sit but their only recorded interest in colonial affairs concerned New England. From 1645 to 1648 they became involved in the controversy over the Narragansett country, and in the attempt of Massachusetts to thwart her enemies, the Gortonists and the Presbyterians.[34] Whether the commission continued to sit after the execution of the King is uncertain; there are no further references to its existence. That many of its members remained influential in colonial affairs is evident from the fact that at least seven of the commissioners became members of the Council of State, appointed February 13, 1649: Philip, Earl of Pembroke (died 1650); Sir Arthur Haslerigg, Sir Harry Vane, the younger; Oliver Cromwell, Dennis Bond, Miles Corbet, and Cornelius Holland. Haslerigg was a conspicuous leader in colonial as well as other matters during the entire period of the Commonwealth and the Protectorate; Vane became president of the new board of trade created in August, 1650, was at the head of the Committee of the Admiralty, which often had colonial matters referred to it, and served frequently on plantation committees from 1649 to 1659; while Bond, Corbet, and Holland, though never very active, were members of one general and a few special committees that concerned themselves with trade and plantations. Thus the spirit of the Independent wing of the old commission continued to influence the policy of the government in the early years of the Commonwealth period. The Council of State, appointed by act of the Rump Parliament, was given full authority to provide for England's trade at home and abroad and to regulate the affairs of the plantations. Though its membership underwent yearly changes and its composition and members were altered many times before 1660, its policy and machinery of control remained constant except as far as they were affected by the greater power which the Council gained in the face of the growing weakness of Parliament.

---

[34] Osgood, The Colonies in the Seventeenth Century, III, pp. 110–112.

CHAPTER II.

CONTROL OF TRADE AND PLANTATIONS DURING THE INTERREGNUM.

The Council of Trade, 1650–1653

The earliest separate council to be established during the period from 1650 to 1660 was that appointed by act of Parliament, August, 1650, known as the Commission or Council of Trade, of which Sir Harry Vane was president and Benjamin Worsley, a London merchant and "doctor of physic," already becoming known as an expert on plantation affairs, was secretary. This body was specially instructed by Parliament to consider, not only domestic and foreign trade, the trading companies, manufactures, free ports, customs, excise, statistics, coinage and exchange, and fisheries, but also the plantations and the best means of promoting their welfare and rendering them useful to England. "They are to take into their consideration," so runs article 12 of the instructions, "the English plantations in America or elsewhere, and to advise how these plantations may best be managed and made most useful for the Commonwealth, and how the commodities thereof may be so multiplied and improved as (if it be possible) those plantations alone may supply the Commonwealth of England with whatsoever it necessarily wants." These statesmanlike and comprehensive instructions are notable in the history of the development of England's commercial and colonial program. Free from the limitations which characterize the instructions given to the earlier commissions, they stand with the Parliamentary ordinance of October, 1650, and the Navigation Act of 1651, as forming the first definite expression of England's commercial policy. Inadequate though the immediate results were to be, we cannot call that policy "drifting" which could shape with so much intelligence the functions of a board of trade and plantations. There is no trace here of the coercive and politico-ecclesiastical purpose of the Laud Commission, or of the partisan policy in the interests of the Puritans that the Warwick Commission was instructed to carry out. Here we have the first attempt to establish a legitimate control of commercial and colonial affairs, and to these instructions may be traced the beginnings of a policy which had the prosperity and wealth of England exclusively at heart.

Of the history of this board but little has been hitherto known and its importance has been singularly neglected. It was more than a merely advisory body, like the later councils and boards of trade, for it had the power to issue orders of its own. It sat in Whitehall, received information, papers,[35] and orders from the

---

[35] Among others, The Advancement of Merchandize or certain propositions for the

Council of State, and reported to that higher authority, which approved or disapproved of its recommendations. To it the Council instructed traders and others to refer their petitions, and itself referred numbers of similar papers that came into its hands.[36] This board took into consideration the various questions touched upon in its instructions, especially those concerning fisheries (Greenland), manufactures, navigation, commerce, trade (with Guinea, Spain, Canary Islands, etc.), the poor, the trading companies (especially the East India and Guinea companies), the merchant companies (chiefly of London), and freedom of trade. During the first year of its existence it was an active body and could say on November 20, 1651, that it had made seven reports to the Council of State and seven to Parliament, that it had its opinions on six subjects ready to be reported, and eight other questions under debate.[37] In two particulars a fuller consideration of its work is desirable.

The Council of Trade devoted a considerable amount of time to regulating the buying and selling of wool, and to settling the difficulties that had arisen among the curriers, fellmongers, staplers, and clothiers of London and elsewhere regarding their trade privileges. Late in the spring of 1651 petitions and statements of grievance had been sent both to the Council of Trade and to the Common Council of London by the "freemen of the city trading in wool," for redress of grievances practiced by the Society of Staplers. Shortly afterward, May 13, apparently in answer to the complaint of the freemen of London, the fellmongers of Coventry petitioned the Council of Trade, begging that body not to interfere with its ancient privileges. Taking the matter into consideration, the Council, on May 14, issued an order requiring the companies to present their expedients and grievances, and appointed a committee of two expert wool staplers, members of the Staplers Company, to meet with the other companies and draft a certificate of their proper and ancient rights. The Common Council, on the same day, ordered its committee of trade, or any five of them, to attend the Council of Trade and assist the "Company of Upholders," the committee presenting the original complaint, in its attempt to obtain a redress of grievances according to the plan already placed before the Common Council. These efforts were not very successful, for the wool growers refused to meet the committee of staplers appointed by the Council of Trade, and the fellmongers and clothiers could not reach an agreement with the staplers as to the latter's ancient privileges. Consequently, the Council of Trade, on June 11, issued a second order requiring the committee of trade of the Common Council to report on "the foundation and nature of the Staple and the privileges pretended to by that Society." This committee "heard certain of the principal staplers and perused

improvement of the trade of this Commonwealth, humbly presented to the Right Honorable the Council of State by Thomas Viollet, of London, Goldsmith, 1651. This rare pamphlet was drawn up by Viollet when connected with the Mint in the Tower and sent to the Council of State, evidently in manuscript form. Most of the papers composing this pamphlet were transmitted by the Council of State to the Council of Trade. For Viollet see Cal. State Papers, Domestic, 1650–1651, 1659–1660.

[36] The Council of Trade accumulated in this and other ways a considerable mass of books and papers, but this material for its history has entirely disappeared.

[37] Cal. State Papers, Dom., 1650, p. 399; 1651, pp. 16, 29, 38, 107, 230; 1651–1652, pp. 87. The first suggestion of this committee was as early as January 1650, Commons' Journal, VI, p. 347.

the acts and records produced by them in defence of the same," and reported to the Council of Trade on June 26 that, in its opinion, the Company of Staplers had become an unnecessary and useless Society, and were the principal cause for the dearness of wool, the badness of cloth, and the general decay of the woolen trade.[38]

The trouble seems to have been that the fellmongers and staplers were deemed useless middlemen between the growers and the clothiers, and injurious to the clothing industry because of their abuses. The controversy was carried before the Council of State and its committees, and both fellmongers and staplers argued long and forcibly in defence of their trade.[39] On November 3, 1652, the two societies presented an answer to the particular order of the Council of Trade which declared them unnecessary and disadvantageous, denied the charges, and prayed that they might enjoy their trade as before. Even as late as April 16, 1653, the fellmongers petitioned for leave to produce wool-growers and clothiers to certify the necessity of their trade.[40] But fellmongers and staplers as factors in English trade and industry were beginning to pass away by the middle of the seventeenth century.

The second important question that came before the Council was no less significant in its relation to the growth of British trade than was the decay of the Societies of Fellmongers and Staplers. It concerned the breaking down of the privileges of the merchant companies in general, and the establishment of free ports and free trade in England—that is, free trade controlled and ordered by the state. To this end, the Council appointed a committee of eleven merchants to whom it gave elaborate directions to report on the feasibility of setting apart four free ports to which foreign commodities might be imported without paying customs dues if again exported. These merchants met and drew up a report dated April 26, 1651, and again on May 26 of the same year expressed further opinions on the advisability of the "opening of free ports for trade." "Trade being the basis and well-being of a Commonwealth, the way to obtain it is to make it a free trade and not to bind up ingenious spirits by exemptions and privileges which are granted to some particular companies." In addition to the home merchants, the Council of Trade presented its queries to the merchant strangers and to the Committee for the Affairs of Trinity House, all of whom returned answers. It also made public its desire to consider the appointment of "convenient ports for the free trade in the Commonwealth," and as early as May 22 a number of the out-ports, Dover, Plymouth, the Isle of Wight, Barnstaple, Bideford, Appledore, and Southampton petitioned that they be recognized as free landing places. The period was one of rivalry between London and the out-ports, and the latter believed that the various acts of 1650 and 1651 were in the interest of the London merchants only. "Yet thus much that act seems to have on it only a London stamp and a contentment to subject the whole nation to them, for most of the out-ports are not capable of the foreign trade to Indies and Turkey. The Londoners having the sole trade do set what price they please upon their commodities, knowing the country cannot have them nowhere but by

[38] Guildhall, Journal of the Proceedings of the Common Council, Vol. 41, ff. 45, 55; Cal. State Papers, Dom., 1651, pp. 198, 247–249, 270–271; Inderwick, The Interregnum, ch. II.

[39] Cal. State Papers, Dom., 1651–1652, pp. 470–472, 479–481.

[40] Cal. State Papers, Dom., 1652–1653, p. 282.

them, whereby not only the out-ports are undone but the country brought to the devotion of the city. But a great abuse is here, for the city are not contented with this act but only so far as it serves their own turns, for they procure (upon some pretexts or other) particular licenses for many prohibited commodities contrary to that act, as namely for the importation of French wines and free both of custom and excise tax, and for the importation of whale oil and skins so as either directly or indirectly they will have the whole trade themselves."[41] Evidently the Council of Trade favored the establishment of a freer trade as against the monopoly of the merchant companies, believing, it may be, that London did monopolize trade and that it was "no good state of a body to have a fat head and lean members." The city authorities, apparently alarmed at the favorable action of the Council, took immediate action. On June 19, 1651, the Court of Aldermen instructed Alderman Fowke, one of its most influential members, in case the Council of Trade came to an agreement favorable to free trade, to move for a reconsideration in order that London might have a hearing before the matter was finally settled.[42] But the hearing, if had, could not have been successful in altering the determination of the Council, for a few months later, on December 5, 1651, the Common Council of London, probably convinced that the Council of Trade was in earnest in its policy and alarmed at the prospect of losing its trading privileges, ordered its committee of trade to prepare a petition to Parliament, the Council of State, or the Council of Trade, asking that London be made a free port. The petition was duly drawn up and approved by the Common Council, which ordered its committee "to maintain" it before the Council of Trade.[43] Evidently the matter went no further. The Council of Trade continued its sittings and debated and reported on a number of petitions "complaining of abuses and deceits" in trade, but after 1652 it plays but an inconspicuous part. Even before that date many questions before it were taken over by the Council of State and referred to its own committees. Fellmongers and staplers defended their cause before the higher body and the free trade difficulty continued to be agitated, at least as far as concerned the Turkey trade and the Greenland fishing, by the Council committee after it had passed out of the hands of the lesser body.[44] The period was one of transition from a monopolized to an open trade, and consequently to many trade everywhere appeared to be in decay. Remedies were sought through the intervention of the state and the passing of laws, but the early period of the Commonwealth was not favorable to a successful carrying out of so promising an experiment. On October 3, 1653, trade was reported from Holland as "somewhat dead" and the Council of Trade, which the Dutch at first feared might be "very prejudicial" to their state, was declared "only nominal," so that the Dutch hoped that in time those of London would "forget that they

[41] British Museum, Add. MSS., 5138, f. 145.

[42] Guildhall, Repertories of the Court of Aldermen, 61, p. 152[b].

[43] Guildhall, Journal of the Proceedings of the Common Council, Vol. 41, pp. 67[b], 68.

[44] Cal. State Papers, Dom., 1651–1652, pp. 232, 235. The question was as to whether or not the Turkey trade could best be carried on by a company "as now," or by free trade, as in the case of Portugal and Spain. Able arguments in favor of free trade were brought forward, and when later the question of a monopoly of the Greenland whale fishing came up, the Council of State admitted free adventurers to a share in the business. Cal. State Papers, Dom., 1653–1654, p. 379; 1654, p. 16.

ever were merchants." In fact, however, the Council of Trade had come to an end more than four months before this report was made.

Plantation Affairs controlled by the Council of State, 1649–1651

That the Council of Trade, notwithstanding its carefully worded instructions, had no part in looking after the affairs of the colonies is probably due to the activity of the Council of State, which itself exercised the functions of a board of trade and plantations. According to article 5 of the Act of February 13, 1649, appointing a Council of State, it was to use all good ways and means for the securing, advancement, and encouragement of the trade of England and Ireland and the dominions to them belonging, and to promote the good of all foreign plantations and factories belonging to the Commonwealth. It was also empowered "to appoint committees of any person or persons for examinations, receiving of informations, and preparing of business for [its] debates or resolutions." The members chosen February 14, 1649, were forty-one in number and were to hold office for one year.[45] February 12, 1650, a second council was elected, of which twenty were new members and the remaining twenty-one taken over from the former body.[46] On November 24, 1651, a third council was chosen under the same conditions.[47] The same was true of the fourth council of November 24, 1652.[48] Many of the "new" members were generally old members dropped for a year or more. On July 9 and 14, 1653, the number of members was reduced to thirty-one, and this council was designed to last only until the following November.[49] Two councils, the fifth and sixth were, therefore, elected in the same year, each composed of fifteen old and fifteen new members. The sixth council, elected November 1, 1653, was chosen for six months, but after six weeks was supplanted by the body known as the Protector's Council, elected December 16, 1653, under the provisions of the *Instrument of Government*.[50] This council was to consist of not more than twenty-one nor less than thirteen members, and according to the method of election provided for in that instrument, was practically controlled by Cromwell himself. The membership varied from time to time, rarely numbering more than sixteen, with an average attendance of about ten. Cromwell was frequently absent from its meetings, but the council, though designed constitutionally to be a check upon his powers, was in reality his ally and answerable to him alone, particularly after the dissolution of Parliament in January, 1655. The council provided for in *The Humble Petition and Advice* was but a continuation of the Protector's Council, so that from December, 1653, until May, 1659, the Protector's Council, representing Cromwell policy and interest, continued to exist. After the abdication of Richard Cromwell and the restoration of the Rump Parliament, the Protector's Council came to an end, and a new council, the eighth, was chosen on May 13, 14, 15, 1659.[51] This body con-

---

[45] Commons' Journal, VI, p. 140.

[46] Commons' Journal, VI, p. 361.

[47] Commons' Journal, VII, p. 41.

[48] Commons' Journal, VII, p. 220.

[49] Commons' Journal, VII, pp. 283, 284, 285.

[50] Commons' Journal, VII, pp. 343–344; Cal. State Papers, Dom., 1653–1654, pp. 297–298.

[51] Commons' Journal, VII, pp. 652, 654, 655; Cal. State Papers, Dom., 1658–1659, p.

tained ten members not of Parliament and lasted until December 31, when a new Council of State was chosen for three months; but on February 21 the council was suspended, and two days afterward the tenth and last council was chosen.[52] On May 21, 1660, this council was declared "not in being," and formally came to an end on May 27, when Charles II, who had had his Privy Council more or less continuously since 1649, named at Canterbury Monck, Southampton, Morrice, and Ashley as privy councillors. The first meeting at Whitehall was held May 31.[53]

The Council of State itself acted as a board of trade and plantations and directly transacted a large amount of business in the interest of manufactures, trade, commerce, and the colonies. It initiated important measures, received petitions, remonstrances, and complaints, either at first hand or through Parliament, from which it also received special orders, entered into debate upon all questions arising therefrom, summoned before it any one who might be able to furnish information or to offer advice, and then drew up its reply, embodied in an order despatched to government officials, private individuals, adventurers, merchant and trading companies, colonial governments in particular or in general. For example, it ordered letters to be written to the plantations, giving them notice of the change of government in 1649, sending them papers necessary for their information, and requiring them to be obedient if they expected the protection which the Republic was prepared to extend to them. Until March 2, 1650, it does not appear to have organized itself especially for this purpose, but on that date it authorized the whole council, or any five members, to sit as a special committee for trade and plantations, and on February 18 and December 2, 1651, repeated the same order.[54] During the early part of this period it depended to a considerable extent on committees, either of merchants and others outside the council, men already engaged in trade with the plantations, such as Worsley, Maurice Thompson (afterward governor of the East India Company), Lenoyre, Allen, Martin Noell, and others, or of councillors forming committees of trade (sitting in the Horse Chamber in Whitehall), of plantations, of the admiralty, of the navy, of examinations, of Scottish and Irish affairs, and of prisoners, to whom many questions were referred and upon whose reports the Council acted. It also appointed special committees to take into consideration particular questions relating to individual plantations, Barbadoes, Somers Islands, Bermudas, New England, Newfoundland, Virginia. Of all these committees none appears to have been more active, as far as the plantations were concerned, than the Committee of the Admiralty, before whom came a large amount of colonial business, which was transacted with the coöperation of Dr. Walker, of Doctors Commons, advocate for the Republic, and David Budd, the proctor of the Court of Admiralty.

349.

[52] Commons' Journal, VII, pp. 800, 849.

[53] P. C. R., Charles II, Vol. I, May 3/13, 1649—September 28, 1660. Meetings of Privy Councils during the Interregnum were held at Castle Elizabeth, St. Hillary, Breda (1649–1650), Bruges (1656, 1658), Brussels (1659), Breda (1660), Canterbury (May 27, 1660), Whitehall (May 31, 1660).

[54] Cal. State Papers, Col., 1574–1660, pp. 335, 352, 366; Cal. State Papers, Dom., 1651–1652, p. 43.

Standing Committee of the Council for Plantations, 1651–April, 1653

Plantation Affairs controlled by the Council of State, April–Dec., 1653

An important departure was introduced on December 17, 1651, when a standing committee of the Council was created, consisting of fifteen members, to concern itself with trade and foreign affairs. This committee took the place of that which had formerly sat in the Horse Chamber in Whitehall, and renewed consideration of all questions which had been referred to that body. It was organized, as were all the Council committees, with its own clerk, doorkeeper, and messenger, and as recommissioned on May 4, 1652, and again on December 2, 1652, when the membership was raised to twenty-one and the plantations were brought within the scope of its business, became a very independent and active body until its demise in April, 1653. Its members were Cromwell, Lords Whitelocke, Bradshaw, and Lisle, Sir Arthur Haslerigg, Sir Harry Vane, Sir William Masham, Sir Gilbert Pickering, Colonels Walton, Purefoy, Morley, Sidney, and Thomson, Major Lister, Messrs. Bond, Scott, Love, Challoner, Strickland, Gurdon, and Alleyn.[55] This committee, to which new members were frequently added, sat in the Horse Chamber at Whitehall and took cognizance of a great variety of commercial and colonial business. It considered the question of free trade versus monopolies and during the summer of 1652, after the Council of Trade had fallen into disfavor, debated at length the desirability of opening the Turkey trade as freely to adventurers as was that of Portugal and Spain. It listened to a number of forcible papers presented in the interest of free trade in opposition to trade in the hands of companies; it dealt with the operation of the Navigation Act of 1651 and rendered decisions regarding penalties, exemptions, licenses, and the disposal of prizes and prize goods; it devoted a large amount of time to plantation business; and, for the time being, probably supplanted consideration of these matters by the Council of State, and rendered unnecessary the appointment of any other committee on colonial affairs. Except for the Admiralty Committee and one or two other committees to which special matters were referred, as concerning Newfoundland, there appears to have been no other subordinate body actually in charge of affairs in America between December 17, 1651, and April 15, 1653. The period was an important and critical one, and the committee must have had before it business connected with nearly every one of the colonies in America. The Council of State referred to it petitions, etc., from and relating to Massachusetts, Plymouth, New Haven, Rhode Island, Newfoundland, Maryland and Virginia, Barbadoes, Nevis, Providence Island, and the Caribbee Islands in general. It dealt with the proposed attack on the Dutch at New Amsterdam, losses of merchant ships, privateer's commissions and letters of marque; the Greenland and Newfoundland fisheries, naval stores, and land disputes. It drafted bills and governors' commissions, considered vacancies in the colonies, and received applications for office, and, in one case, promoted the founding of a plantation in South America.[56] This business was performed to a considerable extent through subcommittees, many of which met in the little Horse Chamber and acted in all particulars as regular committees. On one occa-

[55] Cal. State Papers, Col., 1574–1660, p. 394; Cal. State Papers, Dom., 1651–1652, pp. 67, 232, 235, 426; 1652–1653, pp. 18–27.

[56] Cal. State Papers, Col., 1574–1660, pp. 373–402, *passim*.

sion, the entire committee was appointed a subcommittee, and very frequently the committee met for no other purpose than to hear the report of a subcommittee. These subcommittees, which were generally composed of councillors, referred matters to outside persons, merchants, judges, and doctors of civil law, while the committee itself called before it merchants, officials, members of other committees, and indeed any one from whom information might be extracted. The main work was performed by the subcommittees, their reports were reviewed by the committee itself, and, if approved, were sent to the Council of State, which based upon them recommendations to Parliament.[57] After April 15, 1653, we hear no more of this committee. There is some reason to think that the duties entrusted to it were deemed too extensive and a division between trade, plantations, and foreign affairs was planned, but no definite record of such a separation of functions is to be found. A Council Committee of Foreign Affairs was appointed, probably before June, 1653, reappointed on July 27, and again reappointed August 16, but no committees of trade and of plantations appear. Very likely the Council of State, with the assistance of the committees on Scottish and Irish affairs, admiralty, navy, and customs, and a few special committees and commissioners, assumed control of plantation affairs. The interests of industry and trade may have been looked after by the Committee on Trade and Corporations appointed by the Barebones Parliament, July 20, 1653, "to meet at Whitehall in the place where the Council of Trade did sit."[58] Several times during the year this committee proposed the establishment of a separate council of trade to take the place of the former Council, to which proposition Parliament agreed, but nothing was done, and the Parliamentary Committee of Trade and Corporations seems to have been the only official body that existed during the year 1653 for the advancement of trade and industry.[59]

Trade controlled by Council of State and Parliamentary Committees, Dec., 1653–June, 1655

Importance of the years 1654–1655

On December 29, 1653, the Protector's Council made known its purpose of taking "all care to protect and encourage navigation and trade," and in March, 1654, we meet with a reference to a committee of the Council appointed for trade and corporations. As this body was organized for continuous sitting, with a clerk, doorkeeper, and messenger, and as a second reference to it appears under date August 21, 1654, the probabilities are in favor of its existence as a regular committee during the year 1654.[60] That it was an important committee is doubtful, for we meet with practically no references to its work, and when in January, 1655, the project of a select trade committee was brought forward it was referred for consideration and report, not to this committee, but to Desborough of the Council and the Admiralty Committee.

[57] Cal. State Papers, Dom., 1651–1652, pp. 266, 350, 396, 472; 1652–1653, pp. 18, 27, 160, 171.

[58] Commons' Journal, VII, pp. 19, 287. On May 6, 1653, a new commission of trade was proposed by the Council of State but no appointments are given. Cal. State Papers, Dom., 1653–1654, pp. 310, 344.

[59] Commons' Journal, VII, pp. 308, 319, 341, 375.

[60] Cal. State Papers, Dom., 1654, pp. 61, 285, 316.

The events of the years 1654 and 1655 mark something of an era in the history of trade and commerce, not because the capture of Jamaica had any very conspicuous effect upon Cromwell's own policy or upon the commercial activities of the higher authorities, but because it opened a larger world and larger opportunities to the merchants and traders of London who were at this time seeking openings for trading ventures in all parts of the world. To better their fortunes many men accompanied the expedition under Penn and Venables, and the merchants at home were seized with something of the spirit of the Elizabethans in planning, not only to increase commerce and swell their own fortunes, but also to drive the Spaniard from the southwestern waters of the Atlantic and extend British control and British trade into regions heretofore wholly in the hands of Spain. Barbadoes, Jamaica, Florida, Virginia, New England, Nova Scotia, and Newfoundland became a world of great opportunities, and with plans for the expansion of trade went plans for naval and military activity. If the merchants of the period had had their way, a systematic and orderly policy of colonial control in the interest of British power and profit would have been inaugurated during the second period of the Interregnum, but circumstances do not appear to have been propitious, and the disturbed political order during the years 1658 and 1659 led not only to a cessation of activity as far as the government was concerned but also to decay of trade, shrinking of profits, decrease of fortunes, and widespread discouragement. Furthermore, there is nothing to show that Cromwell himself ever rose to a statesmanlike conception of colonial control and administration. He was thoroughly interested in those matters, was personally influenced by the London merchants, frequently called on the most conspicuous of them for advice, placed them on committees and councils established for purposes of trade, and was always open to their suggestions. But while he was willing to act upon their opinions and recommendations in many respects, he never seems to have grasped the essentials of a large and comprehensive plan of colonial control, and it is not possible to discover in what he actually accomplished any broadminded idea of uniting the colonies under an efficient management for the purpose of laying the foundations of an empire. His expedients, interesting and practical as many of them were, do not seem to be a part of any large or well-formed plan. Whether he would ever have risen to a higher level of statesmanship in these respects we cannot say, but he never found time to give proper attention to the suggestions of the merchants or to the demands of trade and commerce.

The great Trade Committee, 1655–1657

That he took a great interest in the industrial and commercial development of England is evident from one of his earliest efforts to provide for its proper control. Even while the fleet was on its way to the West Indies, the Council of State instructed Desborough and the Admiralty Committee, January 29, 1655, to consider "of some fit merchants to be a trade committee." There is some reason to think that this instruction was in response to a paper drawn up by certain merchants of London in 1654, entitled, "An Essaie or Overture for the regulating the Affairs of his Highness in the West Indies," drafted after the expedition had sailed and with the confident expectation of conquest in mind.[61] If the original suggestion did not come from the merchants, we may not doubt that in the promotion of the plan they exercised considerable influence. In 1655, Martin Noell and Thomas Povey sent a petition to the Protector regarding trade, and suggested that there be appointed "some able persons to consider what more may be done in order to those affairs and a general satisfaction for the fixing the whole trade of England." They wished that a competent number of persons, of good reputation, prudent and well skilled in their professions and qualifications should be "selected and set apart" for the "care of his Highness Affairs in the West Indies." The number was to be not less than seven, and these not to be "of the same but of a mixt qualification," constituting a select council subordinate only to the Protector and the Council. After careful attention to the fitness of a large number of prominent individuals, a committee of twenty was named on July 12, 1655. If the "Overture" was responsible for the decision to name a select council, its influence went no further, for except that merchants were placed as members, there is no likeness between the plan as finally worked out and that formulated by the merchants. Indeed, Povey himself later expressed his dissatisfaction in saying that "that committee which [we] so earnestly prest should be settled will not tend in any degree to what we proposed, the constitution of it being not proportionable to what was desired."[62] The committee of twenty was soon expanded into a much larger and more imposing body, possibly due to the receipt of the news of the capture of Jamaica and the decision announced in Cromwell's proclamation of August to hold the island. On November 11, 1655,[63] a board, made up of officers of state, gentlemen, and merchants, was commissioned a "Committee and Standing Council for the advancing and regulating the Trade and Navigation of the Commonwealth," generally shortened to "Trade and Navigation Committee," or simply "Trade Committee." Its membership, instead of being seven, was over seventy, and it was thus a dignified though unwieldy body. At its head was Richard Cromwell and its members were as follows: Montague, Sydenham, Wolseley, Pickering, and Jones of the Protector's Council; Lord Chief Justice St. John and Justices Glynn, Steele, and Hale; Sir Henry Blount, Sir John Hobart, Sir Gilbert Gerard, gentlemen of distinction; Sir Bulstrode Whitelocke and Sir Thomas Widdrington, sergeants-at-law; Col. John Fiennes and John Lisle, commissioners of the Great Seal; the four Treasury Commissioners; Col. Richard Norton, governor of Portsmouth; Capt. Hatsell, navy commissioner of Plymouth; Stone and Foxcroft, excise commissioners; Martin Noell, London merchant and farmer of the customs; Upton, customs commissioner; Bond, Wright, Thompson, Ashurst, Peirpont, Crew, and Berry, London merchants; and Tichborne, Grove, Pack (Lord Mayor), and Riccards, aldermen of London; Bonner, of Newcastle; Dunne, of Yarmouth; Cullen, of Dover; Jackson, of Bristol; Toll, of

[61] Brit. Mus. Add. MSS., 11411, ff. 11b–12b.

[62] That such an outcome was anticipated is evident from the concluding words of the "Overture." "If his Highness shall think fit to constitute a council for the general Trade of these Nations and the several Interests relating thereunto, these seaven may properly be of that number, the employment being of the same nature and therefore will rather informe then divert them who ought indeed to be busyed or conversant in no other Affaires than the matters of Trade."

[63] Cal. State Papers, Dom., 1655, pp. 27, 133, 240.

Lyme; Legay, of Southampton; Snow, of Exeter; and Drake, of Sussex. At various times, and probably for various purposes, the following members were added between December 12, 1655, and June 19,1656: Secretary Thurloe, William Wheeler, Edmund Waller, Francis Dincke, of Hull; George Downing, at that time major general and scoutmaster; Alderman Ireton, of London; Col. William Purefoy; Godfrey Boseville; Edward Laurence; John St. Barbe, of Hampshire, [Lord] John Claypoole, Master of the Horse, and Cromwell's son-in-law; John Barnard; Sir John Reynolds; Col. Arthur Hill; George Berkeley; Capt. Thomas Whitegreane; Thomas Ford, of Exeter; Francis St. John; Henry Wright; Col. John Jones, Alderman Frederick, sheriff of London; Richard Ford, the well-known merchant of London; Mayor Nehemiah Bourne; Charles Howard; Robert Berwick; John Blaxton, town clerk of Newcastle; Col. Richard Ingoldsby; Edmund Thomas; Thomas Banks, and Christopher Lister. Thus the Trade Committee, composed of members from all parts of England, represented a wide range of interests. Furthermore, any member of the Protector's Council could come to the meetings of the committee and vote.[64] Such a body would have been very unmanageable but for the fact that seven constituted a quorum and business was generally transacted by a small number of the members. The instructions were prepared by Thurloe after a scrutiny of those of the former Council of Trade, and bore little resemblance to the recommendations of the "Overture," because they were designed to cover a far wider range of interests than were considered by the merchants. The "Overture" was planned only for a plantation council. The Trade Committee was invested with power and authority to consider by what means the traffic and navigation of the Republic might best be promoted and regulated, to receive propositions for the benefit of these interests, to send for the officers of the excise, the customs, and the mint, or such other persons of experience as they should deem capable of giving advice on these subjects, to examine the books and papers of the Council of Trade of 1650, and all other public papers as might afford the members information. When finally its reports were ready for the Council of State, that body reserved to itself all power to reject or accept such orders as it deemed proper and fitting.

The Trade Committee met for the first time on December 27, 1655, in the Painted Chamber at Westminster. Authorized to appoint officers, it chose William Seaman secretary, two clerks, an usher, and two messengers at a yearly salary of £280, with £50 for contingent expenses;[65] and from the entries of the payments ordered to be made to these men for their services, we infer that the board sat from December 27, 1655, until May 27, 1657, exactly a year and a half. During this time it probably accumulated a considerable number of books and papers, though

[64] Thurloe, State Papers, IV, p. 177; British Museum, Add. MSS., 12438, iii; Cal. State Papers, Dom., 1655, p. 240, 1655–1656, pp. 1, 2, 54, 73, 100, 114, 115, 141, 156, 162, 188, 252, 275, 297, 327, 382. "We might speak also of the famed 'Committee of Trade' which has now begun its sessions 'in the old House of Lords.' An Assembly of Dignitaries, Chief Merchants, Political Economists, convened by summons of his Highness; consulting zealously how the Trade of this country may be improved. A great concernment of this commonwealth 'which his Highness is eagerly set upon.' They consulted of 'Swedish copperas' and such like; doing faithfully what they could." Cromwell's Letters and Speeches, II, p. 202.

[65] Cal. State Papers, Dom., 1655–1656, p. 113; 1656–1657, p. 556; 1657–1658, pp. 308, 589; 1657–1658, p. 69.

such are not now known to exist. Proposals, petitions, complaints, and pamphlets, such, for example, as that entitled *Trading Governed by the State*, a protest against the commercial dominance of London, were laid before it, and it took into its own hands many of the problems that had agitated the former board. It discussed foreign trade, particularly with Holland, and the questions of Swedish copper,[66] Spanish wines, and Irish linen; home manufactures, among which are mentioned swords and rapier blades, madder-dyed silk, needle making, and knitting with frameworks; and domestic concerns, such as the preservation of timber. It made a number of recommendations regarding "the exportation of several commodities of the breed, growth, and manufacture of the Commonwealth," "the limiting and settling the prices of wines," "vagrants and wandering, idle, dissolute persons," and the "giving license for transporting fish in foreign bottoms." These recommendations were drafted by the Trade Committee, or by one of its subcommittees, and after adoption were reported to the Council of State and by it referred to its own committee appointed to receive reports from the Trade Committee. When approved by the Council of State, the recommendations were sent to Parliament and there referred to the large Parliamentary committee of trade of fifty members, appointed October 20, 1656. That committee drafted bills which were based on these recommendations and which later were passed as acts of Parliament and received the consent of the Protector. For example, the recommendation regarding exports, noted above, became a law November 27, 1656.[67]

Under the head of "navigation and trade" came the commercial interests of the plantations, and though there existed during this year, 1656, other machinery for regulating plantation affairs, a number of questions were referred from the Council to the Trade Committee that were strictly in the line of plantation development. These questions concerned customs duties on goods exported to Barbadoes, the political quarrels in Antigua which threatened to bring ruin on that plantation and the remedies therefor, the pilchard fishery off Newfoundland, and finally the controversy between Maryland and Virginia which had already been referred to a special committee of the Council. Upon all these questions the Trade Committee reported to the Council; its recommendations and findings were debated in that body or further referred to one of its own committees or to the outside committee for America, and finally embodied in an order regulating the matter in question.[68]

Parliamentary Committees of Trade, 1656–1658

Plantation Affairs controlled by Protector's Council and Council of the State, 1653–1660

Of the activity of the Trade Committee during the few months of the year 1657, when it continued its sessions, scarcely any evidence appears. There is a very slight reason to believe that it took up the question of free ports, but there is nothing to show that it accomplished anything in that direction. That it came to an end in May seems to be borne out by the fact that the officers of the board were paid only to May 27, but this statement is rendered uncertain by the further fact that

[66] Cal. State Papers, Dom., 1655–1656, p. 318.
[67] Commons' Journal, VII, pp. 442, 452, 460.
[68] Cal. State Papers, Col., 1574–1660, pp. 436, 439, 440 (2), 441, 443, 447, 453.

on June 26 Portsmouth petitioned the committee to be made a free port and that the petition was brought in by one of the members of the committee for America, Capt. Limbrey.[69] The question cannot be exactly settled. Though the committee was by no means a nominal body, it accomplished little, and certainly did not meet the situation that confronted the trade and navigation of the kingdom.

After the appointment of this select Trade Committee, no standing committee of the Council was created. Questions of trade were looked after either by the Council itself, that of May, 1659, being especially instructed to "advance trade and promote the good of our foreign plantations and to encourage fishing,"[70] by an occasional special committee, by the Trade Committee until the summer of 1657, or by the committees of Parliament. Of Parliamentary committees there were two: one a select committee of fifty members, appointed October 20, 1656, to which were added all the merchants of the House and all members that served for the port towns;[71] and a grand committee of the whole House for trade, appointed February 2, 1658, which sat weekly and was invested with the same powers as the committee of 1656 had had.[72] But except that the first committee adopted some of the recommendations of the Trade Committee, there is nothing to show that these committees took any prominent part in the advancement of the interest in behalf of which they had been created.

Special Council Committees for Plantations, 1653–1659

Council Committee for Jamaica and Foreign Plantations, 1655–1660

From 1654 to 1660 the welfare of the plantations lay chiefly in the hands of the Protector's Council and the Council of State, and their system of control was in many respects similar to that which had been adopted during the earlier period of the Interregnum. At first all plantation questions were referred to committees of the Council appointed temporarily to consider some particular matter. From December 29, 1653, to the close of the year 1659 some fifty cases were referred to about thirty committees, of which twenty were appointed for the special purpose in hand. Many matters were referred to such standing committees as the Admiralty Committee, Customs Committee, etc.; others to the judges of admiralty, commissioners of customs, and the like, while petitions and communications regarding affairs in Jamaica, New England, Virginia, Antigua, Somers Islands, Newfoundland, and Nevis, regarding the transporting of horses, mining of saltpeter, payments of salaries, indemnities, and trade, and regarding personal claims, such as those of Lord Baltimore, William Franklin, De La Tour, and others, were referred to committees composed of from two to eight members of the Council, whose services in this particular ended with the presentation of their report. Sometimes a question would be referred to the whole Council or to a "committee," with the names unspecified, or to "any three of the Council." The burden of serving upon these occasional committees fell upon a comparatively small number of councillors: Ashley, Montague, Strickland, Wolseley, Fiennes, Jones,

[69] Brit. Mus., Add. MSS., 12438, iii.
[70] Cal. State Papers, Dom., 1658–1659, p. 349.
[71] Commons' Journal, VII, pp. 442, 452.
[72] Commons' Journal, VII, p. 596.

Sydenham, Lisle, and Mulgrave. One or more of these names appear on the list of every special committee appointed except that to which Lord Baltimore's case was referred, consisting of the sergeants-at-law, Lords Whitelocke and Widdrington. During 1654 the committees for Virginia and Barbadoes, to which were referred other colonial matters, came to be known as the "committee for plantations," but it is doubtful if this was deemed in any sense a standing committee.

Select Committee for Jamaica, known later as Committee for America, 1655–1660

When the affairs of Jamaica became exigent after the summer of 1655 a committee of the Council was appointed to carry out the terms of Cromwell's proclamation and to report the needs of the colony. Though the membership was generally changed this committee continued to be reappointed as one question after another arose which demanded the attention of the Council. It reported on the equipment of tools, clothing, medicaments and other necessaries, on the transporting of persons from Ireland and colonies in America, on the distribution of lands in the island, and on various matters presented to the Council in letters and petitions from officers and others there or in England. After 1656 this committee, which continued to exist certainly until the middle of April, 1660, played a more or less secondary part, doing little more than consider the various colonial matters, whether relating to Jamaica or to other colonies, that were taken up by the select or outside committee appointed by Cromwell in 1656.

The employment of expert advisers in the Jamaica business was rendered necessary by the financial questions involved, and in December Robert Bowes, Francis Hodges and Richard Creed were called upon to assist a committee of Council appointed May 10, 1655, in determining the amounts due the wives and assignees of the officers and soldiers in Jamaica. Creed was dropped and Sydenham and Fillingham were added in 1656.[73] But a more important step was soon taken. On July 15, 1656, Cromwell appointed a standing committee of officers and London merchants to take general cognizance of all matters that concerned "his Highness in Jamaica and the West Indies." The following were the members: Col. Edward Salmon, an admiralty commissioner and intimately interested in the Jamaica expedition; Col. Tobias Bridges, one of Cromwell's major generals, afterwards serving in Flanders, who was to play an important part in proclaiming Richard Cromwell Protector; Lieutenant Colonel Miller, of Col. Barkstead's regiment, and Lieutenant Colonel Mills; Capt. Limbrey, London merchant and Jamaican planter, who had lived in Jamaica and made a map of the island, and as commander of merchant vessels had made many trips across the Atlantic; Capt. Thomas Aldherne, also a London merchant and sea captain, the chief victualler of the navy, and an enterprising adventurer in trade; Capt. John Thompson, sea captain and London merchant; Capt. Stephen Winthrop, sea captain and London merchant; Richard Sydenham, and Robert Bowes, already mentioned as commissioners for Jamaica,[74] and lastly Martin Noell, London merchant, and Thomas Povey, regarding whom a fuller account is given below. Povey, who was not appointed a member until October, 1657, apparently became chairman and secretary, while Francis

[73] Cal. State Papers, Dom., 1655–1656, pp. 46, 65, 318, 351.
[74] Cal. State Papers, Dom., 1657–1658, pp. 51, 66.

Hodges was clerical secretary. Except for Tobias Bridges, the military members had little share in the business of the committee, the most prominent part being taken by Noell, Bridges, Winthrop, Bowes, Sydenham, and Povey. As far as the records show, Salmon, Miller, Aldherne, Thompson, and White never signed a report, while Mills and Limbrey signed but one. The committee seems to have sat at first in Grocer's Hall, afterward in Treasury Chambers, where its members discussed and investigated all questions that came before them with care and thoroughness. Their instructions authorized them to maintain a correspondence with the colonies, obtaining such information and advice as seemed essential; to receive all addresses relating thereunto, whether from persons in America or elsewhere; to consider and consult thereof and prepare such advices and answers thereupon as should be judged meet for the advantage of the community. Their earliest business concerned itself with Jamaica, its revenues, finances, expenses of expeditions thither, arrears due the officers and soldiers, their wives and assignees, individual claims, want of ministers, and other similar questions. But as addresses came in from other colonies the scope of their activity was broadened until it included at one time or another nearly all the American colonies. The committee reported on the constitution, governing powers, fortifications, militia of Somers Islands (Bermudas) and on the fitness of Sayle to be governor there; on the controversy between Virginia and Maryland and on the organization and government of the former colony; on the petition of the Long Islanders and others in New England, and on complaints against Massachusetts Bay; on the revenue, government, and admiralty system of Barbadoes; on questions of governor and arrears of salary in Nevis and Tortugas; on the desirability of continuing the plantation in Newfoundland; and lastly on the important subject of ship insurance, upon which Capt. Limbrey presented a very remarkable paper.[75] These reports were sent sometimes to the Protector, sometimes to the Council of State, and sometimes to the committee of the Council on the affairs of America. While the latter committee, under the name of "Committee for Foreign Plantations" continued until the return of the King, the select committee for America does not appear to have lasted as a whole after the final dissolution of the Rump Parliament, March 16, 1660. Thomas Povey alone seems to have been the committee from March to May, and on April 9 and May 11 made two reports on matters referred to him by the Council committee regarding Jamaica and Newfoundland. As Charles II had been recalled to his own in England before the last report was sent in, the machinery created under Cromwell for the plantations remained in existence after the government set up by him had passed away.[76]

---

[75] Cal. State Papers, Col., 1574, 1660, pp. 445, 447, 448, 449, 450, 452, 453, 455, 456, 458, 459, 460, 461, 464, 465, 468, 470, 477; Brit. Mus. Egerton, 2395, ff. 123, 136, 142, 148–151, 157; Add. MSS., 18986, f. 258.

[76] Note to the report of May 11, 1660, is as follows: "By order of the Councill of State sitting and taking care of the government in the interval between the suppression of the Rump of the Parliament and the return of his Majesty which was not many days before the date of this report." Egerton MSS., 2395, f. 263. Probably the recall not the actual landing at Dover is meant.

Inadequacy of Control during the Interregnum

Any account of the system appointed for the control of trade and plantations during the Interregnum is bound to be something of a tangle, not because the system itself was a complicated one, but because its simplicity is clouded by a bewildering mass of details. Occasional committees of Parliament, the Council as a board of trade and plantations, committees of the Council, and select councils and committees do not form a very confusing body of material out of which to fashion a system of colonial control. Yet, despite this fact, the management of the colonies during the Interregnum was without unity or simplicity. Control was exercised by no single or continuous organ and according to no clearly defined or consistent plan. Colonial questions seemed to lie in many different hands and to be met in as many different ways. Delays were frequent and there can be little doubt that many important matters were laid aside and pigeon-holed. When an important colonial difficulty had to pass from subcommittee to committee, from committee to Council, and sometimes from Council to Parliamentary committee and thence to Parliament, we can easily believe that in the excess of machinery there would be entailed a decrease of despatch and efficiency. Indeed, during the Interregnum colonial business was not well managed and there were many to whom colonial trade was of great importance, who realized this fact. Merchants of London after 1655 became dissatisfied with the way the plantations were managed and desired a reorganization which should bring about order, improve administration, economize expenditure, elevate justice, and effect speedily and fairly a settlement of colonial disputes. They doubted whether a Council, "busyed and filled with a multitude of affairs," was able to accomplish these results and they refused to believe that affairs of such a nature should be transacted "in diverse pieces and by diverse councils." The remedy of these men was carefully thought out and carefully expressed and though it was undoubtedly listened to by Cromwell, it never received more than an imperfect application. To these men and their proposals we must pay careful attention for therein we shall find the connecting link between the Protectorate and the Restoration as far as matters of trade and the plantations are concerned.

CHAPTER III.

THE PROPOSALS OF THE MERCHANTS: NOELL AND POVEY.

Career of Martin Noell

Between the colonial and commercial activities of the later years of the Interregnum and the corresponding activities during the early years of the Restoration no hard and fast line can be drawn. The policy of control adopted by Charles II can be traced to the agitation of men, chiefly merchants of London and others familiar with the colonies, who since 1655 had become impressed with the possibilities of the New World as a field for profitable ventures in trade and commerce, and desired, whether under a republic or a monarchy, the coöperation and aid of the government. Among the leaders of this movement were Martin Noell and Thomas Povey.

Martin Noell was probably the most conspicuous London merchant of his time. Of his early life nothing seems to be known. He first appears as a merchant in 1650 trading with Nevis and Montserrat, and in the next few years he extended his operations to New England, Virginia, the other West India islands, and the Mediterranean. His ships trafficked in a great variety of commodities—iron, hemp, pitch, tar, flax, potashes, cables, fish, cocoa, tobacco, etc., and he became a power in London, his place of business in Old Jewry being the resort of merchants, ship captains, and persons desiring to coöperate in his ventures. He was an alderman as early as 1651, was placed a little later on the commission for securing the peace of the city, and held other offices by appointment of the city or of the Commonwealth. He was also a member of the East India Company and influential in its councils. In addition to his mercantile interests he became a farmer, first of the inland and foreign post-office,—one writer speaking of him as "the postmaster,"—and later, on a large scale, of customs and excise. At one time or another he held the farm of the customs in general and of the excise of salt, linen, silk mercery, and wines in particular. In these capacities he acted as a banker of the government, paying salaries and expenses of official appointees, advancing loans, and issuing bills of exchange and letters of credit. His vessels carried letters of marque during the Dutch war and the war with Spain, and he himself traded in prizes and became one of the commissioners of prize goods. The Jamaican expeditions of 1654 and afterward gave him an opportunity to become a contractor and he organized a committee in London for the purpose of financiering the expedition, himself advancing £16,000, and in company with Capts. Alderne, Watts, and others contracted for the supplies of the ships and soldiers, furnishing utensils, clothing, bedding, and provisions for this and other expeditions, notably that to Flanders. He was Gen. Venables' personal agent in London and agent for the army in general in Jamaica. He also became a contractor for transporting vagrants, prisoners, and others to various American plantations. These accumulating ventures increased his interest in the colonies, and after the capture of Jamaica in 1655 he obtained a grant of 20,000 acres in that island, from which he created several plantations. In his new capacity as planter he was constantly engaged in shipping servants, supplies, and horses. The firm of Martin Noell & Company became exceedingly prosperous, and Noell himself one of the mainstays of the government. He became a member of the Trade Committee in 1655, of the committee for Jamaica in 1656, and was frequently called in by the Council of State to offer advice or to give information. He was on terms of intimacy with Cromwell, and because of the Protector's friendship for him and confidence in his judgment, his recommendations for office, both in England and the colonies had great weight. Povey speaks of the "extraordinary favor allowed him (Noell) by his Highness." He had a brother, Thomas Noell, who was prominent in Barbadoes and Surinam and in charge of his interests there. He was also represented in other islands by agents and factors, of whom Edward Bradbourne was the most conspicuous, while Major Richard Povey in Jamaica, and William Povey in Barbadoes, brothers of Thomas Povey, had for a time charge of his plantations in those islands. Noell indirectly played no small part in politics, particularly of Barbadoes, where Governor Searle held office largely through his influence. Besides his Jamaica holdings he had estates at Wexford in Ireland, and in April, 1658, wrote to Henry Cromwell that he had "transplanted much of his interest and affairs and relations" to that country, seeming to indicate thereby that his colonial ventures were not prospering satisfactorily. Noell was a politic man, shrewd and diplomatic, asserting his loyalty to the house of Cromwell, yet becoming a trusty subject of King Charles, from whom he afterward received knighthood.[77]

Career of Thomas Povey

Thomas Povey was born probably about 1615, son of Justinian Povey, auditor of the exchequer and one of the commissioners of the Caribbee Islands in 1637. He was one of a large family of children, nine at least, Justinian, John, Francis, William, Richard, Thomas, Mrs. Blathwayt (afterward Mrs. Thomas Vivian), Mrs. Barrow, and Sarah Povey, and he spent his early years at the family home in Hounslow. In 1633 he entered Gray's Inn and in 1647 became a member of the Long Parliament. "Purged" with the other Presbyterian members in 1648, he did not return to Parliament until the restoration of those members in 1659. He was evidently inclined at first to go into law and politics, but for reasons unnamed, possibly the slenderness of his fortune, which he says was hardly sufficient to support him, he turned, about 1654, to trade, and was thus brought into close relations with Martin Noell. Of his activities until 1657 we hear very little, though it is evident that from 1654 to 1657 he lived in Gray's Inn, engaging in many trading ventures in the West Indies and elsewhere, was on terms of intimacy with Noell and frequently at his house,

[77] Cal. State Papers, Col., 1574–1660; Dom., vols. for years 1650–1660, Indexes; Brit. Mus. Egerton, 2395, Add. MSS., 11410, 11411, 15858, f. 97, 22920, f. 22; Lansdowne, 822, f. 164, 823, f. 33.

and showed himself fertile of suggestions, as always, regarding the improvement of trade and the care and supply of men, provisions, and intelligence. In 1657 he lost by death his brothers John and Francis, and his mother, who died at Hounslow. As two of his brothers had gone to the West Indies with the expedition of 1654 and the remainer of the family was scattered, he decided to marry, and settled down in a house in Lincoln's Inn Fields next the Earl of Northampton, with a widow without children, but possessed "of a fortune capable of giving a reasonable assistance to mine." In October of that year, possibly through Noell's influence, he became a member of the committee for America, and from that time was a conspicuous leader among those interested in plantation affairs. As chairman and secretary of the committee, he took a prominent part in all correspondence, and was familiar with the chief men in all the colonies. He exchanged letters with Searle, of Barbadoes, D'Oyley, of Jamaica, Temple, of Nova Scotia, Digges, at one time governor of Virginia, Russell, of Nevis, Major Byam, of Surinam, Col. Osborn, of Montserrat, General Brayne, in command of one of the expeditions to Jamaica, and particularly with Lord Willoughby of Parham, with whom he stood on terms of intimate friendship and over whose policy he exercised considerable control. He was proposed at this time as agent in London for Virginia, but the suggestion does not appear to have been acted on. His brother Richard was commissary of musters and major of militia in Jamaica, and his brother William, the black sheep of the family, who had married a wife far too good for him, as Povey once wrote her, was provost marshal in Barbadoes and in charge of Noell's interests there, bringing that merchant nothing but "discontent and damage," and causing Thomas Povey a great deal of trouble and expense. The colonial appointments of these brothers were obtained entirely through the influence of Noell and Povey in England. The disordered and uncertain political situation in England in 1659 and the unsettled state of affairs in both Jamaica and Barbadoes at the same time cost Povey great anxiety and a part of his own and his wife's fortune, and he echoed the complaint, widespread at the time, of the decay of trade and the insecurity of all commercial ventures. We may not doubt that Povey, as well as Noell, was ready to welcome the return of the King.[78]

Enterprises of the Merchants, 1657–1659

Though Noell and Povey were intimate friends and had been engaged in common trading enterprises for a number of years, we have no definite knowledge of their earlier undertakings, beyond the fact that with Capt. Watts and Capt. Aldherne, whom Povey met by accident at Noell's house, they were particularly concerned in developing the Barbadoes and Jamaica trade. In the years 1657 and 1658, when Noell was "swol'n into a much greater person by being a farmer of the customs and excise," we meet with two enterprises, one for a West India Company, promoted by Lord Willoughby, Noell, Povey, and Watts, as partners and principals, with Watts as sea captain in charge of the vessel; the other for a Nova Scotia Company, composed of Lord William Fiennes, Sir Charles Wolseley, Noell, Povey, and others, with Watts and Collier as managers and Capt. Middleton

[78] Cal. State Papers, Col. and Dom. Indexes; Egerton, 2395, which contains Povey's collection of papers; Add. MSS., 11411, which contains his correspondence. See also Dictionary of National Biography.

as sailing master. The latter company was organized for settling a trade in furs and skins in Nova Scotia, and to that end engaged the coöperation of Wolseley's cousin, Col. Thomas Temple, lieutenant general of Nova Scotia since 1655, and of Capt. Breedon, a prominent merchant of New England. It sent out a ship freighted with goods under Capt. Middleton, but despite an auspicious beginning, does not appear to have prospered. The title to Nova Scotia was disputed not only by the French, but also by the Kirkes, whom Cromwell had dispossessed in 1655, when he appointed Temple as governor; hostilities broke out in Nova Scotia, and the company was called upon for a larger stock and incorporation at a time when its promoters seemed unwilling to risk more money. Though Povey was encouraged by the specimens of copper which Temple sent over, the enterprise made no progress until after the Restoration. It is probable that both Noell and Povey lost money by the venture.

The project for a West India Company was more ambitious and must have been formulated some time in 1656 or 1657. Various propositions were drawn up with care, probably by Povey or by Noell and Povey together, for the better serving the interests of the Commonwealth by the erection of a company which had as its object the advancing of trade and the prosecution of the war with Spain. The two ideas seem, however, to have been kept separate. Trade was to be promoted by despatching a vessel to "Florida" under Capt. Watts which, in case it was unable to open trade there, was to take on a lading of pipe staves in New England, sail to the West Indies, and return thence with a cargo of sugar and other West Indian commodities. For the purpose of attacking Spanish towns, of "interrupting the Spanish fleet in their going from Spain to the Indies and in their return thence for Spain, and of ousting the Spaniards from their control in the West Indies and South America" — a subject regarding which Capt. Limbrey had drawn up a paper of information, — the company proposed that the state should furnish and equip twenty frigates which were to be fully provisioned, manned and officered by itself. The company desired to be incorporated by act of Parliament,[79] rather than by a patent under the great seal, because the former would confer "diverse privileges and assistances, and an immunity and sole trade in any place they shall conquer or beget a trade with the Spaniard's dominion," all of which a patent could not convey. The proposals were presented to the Council of State in 1659 and were referred to a special committee. They were debated in Council on August 7, and on October 20 Povey wrote to Governor Searle that they had received encouragement and hoped to have a charter from Parliament, and because "they have so much favor from the state they will have an influence upon most of the English plantations."[80] Either Parliament refused to incorporate the company or in the distractions of the winter of 1659–1660 the proposals were lost sight of.

Proposals of Noell and Povey

The group of merchants, among whom Noell and Povey were so conspicuous, seemed to desire, as far as possible, a monopoly of the trade in America and the

---

[79] A draft of such an act is to be found in Egerton, 2395, f. 202.

[80] Brit. Mus. Egerton, 2395, pp. 87–113, 176 (there is a duplicate of Povey's letter in Add. MSS., 11410); Cal. State Papers, Col., 1574–1660, pp. 475, 477.

West Indies, and to that end controlled to no inconsiderable extent political appointments there. Governor Searle, of Barbadoes, was their appointee, and Governors Russell, of Nevis, and Osborn, of Montserrat, were in close touch with them and looked to them for support. In 1657, acting through the committee for America, they recommended that Edward Digges be made governor of Virginia, and about the same time Martin Noell and eighteen others petitioned that Capt. Watts be made governor of Jamaica. Lord Willoughby was practically one of them, and Gen. Brayne and Lieut. Gen. D'Oyley were on intimate terms with them. It is not surprising, in view of the importance of the colonial trade and the disturbed condition of the plantations, that such a man as Povey, who was always ready with plans and proposals, should have endeavored to solve the problem of colonial control. He was in frequent consultation with Noell concerning matters relating to the West Indies, and in consequence, many schemes were discussed and carefully worked out by them. The various drafts touching the West India Company are elaborated in minute detail, and Povey showed clearly that he possessed admirable qualities as a committee-man and an organizer.

"Overtures" of 1654

The first "overture" or plan seems to have been written in 1654 at the time when the expedition of Penn and Venables was on its way to the West Indies, and does not refer specifically to Jamaica. Its authors recommended that a competent number of persons, not less than seven, of good repute and well skilled in their professions and qualifications, be selected to form a council. A greater number would be undesirable, they said, because "in such an affair where there are many, the chief things are done and ofttimes huddled up by a few; and there is neither that secrecy, steadiness, nor particular care, nor so good an account given of the trust, where more are employed than are necessary and proportionable to the business."[81] The qualifications of the seven are interesting: "(1) One to be a Merchant that hath been in those Indias and trading that waie. (2) One also to bee a Merchant but not related to that trade, and who rather retires from than pursues in profession. (3) One well experienced Seaman, not or but little trading att present. (4) One Gentleman that hath travailed; that hath language and something of the civill Lawe. (5) One Citizen of a general capacitie and conversation. (6) One that understands well our municipall Lawes and the general Constitutions of England. (7) One to be a Secretarie to his Highness in all Affaires in the West Indias, and relating thereunto, who is solely to give himself up to this Employm^t." This council was to be subordinated only to Cromwell and the Council and its powers were to be fairly extensive. It was

> "to have power to advise wth all other Committees or Persons, Officers, or others as occasion shall require;
>
> "to consider (by what they shall observe here and what shalbee represented from the Commission^{rs} now in the expedition) how and what forreigne Plantations may be improved, transplanted, and ordered;

---

[81] That all these proposals were drafted by Povey is evident from similar terms and phrases used in his letters.

"to reduce all Colonies and Plantations to a more certaine, civill, and uniforme way of government and distribution of publick justice;

"to keep a constant correspondence with the Commission^{rs} now in the expedition, and wth all the Chiefe Ports both at home and abroad;

"to be able to give up once in a year unto his Highness a perfect Intelligence and Account of the Government of every place, of their complaints, their wants, their abundance of every ship trading thither and its lading and whither consigned, and to know what the proceeds of the place have been that yeare, whereby the intrinsick value and the certaine condition of each port will be thoroughly understood. And by this conduct and method those many rich places and severall Governments and Adventures will have all due and continuall care and Inspection taken of them, wthout divertion to the nearest Affairs of this Nation, wch being of so much of a greater and a closer consequence, the Superior Council can seldome bee at leisure to descend any further than to breife and imperfect considerations and provisions, wch is the sad Estate of fforeigne Dominions, and distant Colonies and Expeditions from whence usually the most strict, or servile duty and obedience is exacted, but very seldome any Indulgencie or paternall care is allowed to them.

"These therefore are to indeavour and contrive all possible Encouragem^{ts} and Advantages for the Adventurer, Planter, and English Merchants, in order also to the shutting out all Straingers from that Trade, by making them not necessary to it, and by drawing it wholly and with satisfaction to all parties into our Ports here, that it may bee afterward instead of Bullion to trade with other Nations, it being the Traffick of our own proper and native Commodities. That our Shipping may be increased, our poore here employed, and our Manufactures encouraged: And by the generall consequencies hereof, a considerable Revenue may be raised to his Highness.

"to debate among themselves, and satisfy themselves from others; and to present their Results to his Highness in all matters reserved and proper for his Highness Judgment and last Impressions.

"to bee a readie and perfect Register both to his Highness and all other persons, as far as they may be concerned, of all particulars relating to those Affaires.

"The Secretarie may be the person to represent things from time to time between his Highness and this Councill. To make and receive dispatches. To make readie papers for his Highness signature. And generally his Office wilbee to render the Supreame Management & comp^rhension of this Affaire less cumbersome and difficult to his Highness, hee being allwaies ready to give his Highness a full and a digested consideration, if any particular re- lating to those Affaires and wth in the cognizance of that Council."[82]

"Queries" of 1656

That these recommendations had any influence in determining the character of the Trade Committee of 1655 is doubtful, but the next effort of the merchants was probably more successful. Some time in 1656 Povey drew up a series of que- ries "concerning his Highness Interest in the West Indias" in which occur the fol- lowing suggesive paragraphs:

"Whether a Councell busyed and filled with a multitude of Affaires, wch concerne the imediat Safety and preservation of the State at home, can bee thought capable of giving a proper conduct to such various and distant Interests.

"Whether an Affaire of such a nature and consequence may be transacted in diverse peices and by diverse Councells, and how a proper Result cann be instantly arise out of such a kind of man- agement.

"Whether a Councill constituted of fitt Persons Solely sett apart to the busyness of America be not the likeliest means of ad- vancing his Highness Interest there and of bringing them contin- ually to a certain account and readiness whensoever his Highness or his Privie Councill shall have occasion to looke into any partic- ular thereof.

"Whether it be not a prudentiall thing to draw all the Islands, Colonies, and Dominions of America under one and the same management here."[83]

That the men who drafted these queries were mainly responsible for the cre- ation of the select council of 1656, at first known as the Committee for Jamaica and afterwards as the Committee for his Highness Affairs in America, we can hardly doubt, for the constitution and work of that committee represents very nearly the ideas that Povey and Noell had expressed up to this time. It is not to be wondered at that Povey should have been the chairman, secretary, and most active member of this committee after his appointment in 1657.

Additional Proposals, 1656, 1657

Two other propositions or overtures appear among Povey's papers that be- long to the period of the Protectorate, and were written probably the one in 1656, known as the "Propositions concerning the West India Councill," and the other, known as "Overtures touching the West Indies," before August, 1657.[84] In the first

---

[82] Brit. Mus., Add. MSS., 11411, ff. 11^b–12^b.

[83] Brit. Mus., Egerton, 2395, f. 86.

[84] Brit. Mus., Egerton, 2395, f. 99; Add. MSS., 11411, ff. 3–3^b. In a letter of August, 1657,

of these the number of the council was to be ten, in the second it was not to exceed six. The "Propositions" repeat in the main the points already quoted, including the recommendation that it should be the business of the council "to consider of the reducing all Colonies and Plantations to a more certaine, civill, and uniform waie of Governm^t and distribution of publick justice." The "Overtures" are much more elaborate, though frequently containing the identical phrases of the first "Overture," with many new paragraphs which seem to show the same spirit of hostility for Spain that is exhibited in the formation of the West India Company. Indeed this document is an outcome of the same movement which led to the formation of that company. Some of the more important sections are as follows:

"To render what we already possess, and all that depends upon it, to be a foundation and Inducem^t for future undertakings; by gathering reasonable assistances from thence, and by mingling and interweaving of Interest, and letting it appear that such Persons and Collonies shall have the more of the Indulgencie of the State as shall merit most in what they shall in any way be readier to do, or contribut to the service of the whole; for hereafter they may be considered as one embodied Commonwealth whose head and centre is here.

"That every Governour shall have his Commission reviewed, and that all be reviewed in one form, wth such clauses and provisions as shalbee held necessary for the promotion of his Highness other public affairs, and that as soone as order can be conveniently taken therein the several Governours to be paid their allowances from hence (though upon their own accounts), that their dependencie bee immediately and altogether from his Highness....

"That all prudentiall means be applyed to for the rendering these Dominions useful to England, and England helpful to them; and that the severall Peices and Colonies bee drawn and disposed into a more certaine, civill, and uniforme waie of Government and distribution of Publick Justice. And that such Collonies as are the Proprietie of particular Persons or of Corporations may be reduced as neare as cann bee to the same method and proportion wth the rest wth as little dissatisfaction or injurie to the persons concerned as may bee.

"That a continual correspondence bee so settled and ordered ... that so each place wthin itself and all of them being as it were made up into one Commonwealth may be regulated accordingly upon comon and equal Principles."

These proposals are followed by a series of propositions designed to further the enterprise of the merchants and to aid in the defeat of the Spaniards, whereby "those oppressed People (who are wthheld from Trade though to their extreme

Povey refers to these "Overtures," which he says were designed "for the better setting and carrying on of the general affairs of the West Indies, enforcing the authority and powers of the several governors there, and the establishment of a certain course," etc.

suffering and disadvantage)" may be released "from the Tyranny [of Spain] now upon them."

Taken as a whole, these documents form a remarkable series of unofficial papers which formulate foundation principles of colonial empire that England never applied. That these principles met the approval of those who were to shape the colonial policy of the Restoration a further examination will show.

CHAPTER IV.

COMMITTEES AND COUNCILS UNDER THE RESTORATION.

Plantation Committee of Privy Council, June 4, 1660

Charles II landed at Dover on May 25, 1660 and on the twenty-seventh named at Canterbury four men, General Monck, the Earl of Southampton, William Morrice, and Sir Anthony Ashley Cooper, who took oath as privy councillors. Others who had been members of the Council on foreign soil or were added during the month following the return of the King swelled the number to more than twenty. The first meeting of the Privy Council was held on May 31, and it was inevitable that during the ensuing weeks many petitions concerning the various claims and controversies which had been agitating merchants and planters during the previous years and had been reported on by the Committee for America should have been brought to the attention of the Council. Such matters as appointments to governorships and other offices, the political disturbances in Antigua, Barbadoes, and Jamaica, the titles to Nova Scotia, Newfoundland, and Barbadoes, became at once living issues. Many of the petitions were from the London merchants, and we may not doubt that the personal influence of those whose names have been already mentioned was brought to bear upon the members of the Council. It became necessary, therefore, for the King and his advisers to make early provision for the proper consideration of colonial business in order that the colonies might be placed in a position of greater security and in order that the West Indian and American trade, from which the King and his Chancellor expected important additions to the royal revenue, might be encouraged and extended. Among the petitions received in June, 1660, were two from rival groups of merchants interested in the governorship and trade of the island of Nevis. One of these petitions desired the confirmation of the appointment of Col. Philip Ward as governor of Nevis; the other the reappointment of the former governor, Russell. This was the first difficult question that had yet arisen, for Berkeley's return to Virginia was a foregone conclusion, while the condition and settlement of Nova Scotia, Barbadoes and Jamaica were to be of importance later. Acting on these petitions regarding Nevis, only the second of which is entered in the Privy Council Register, the King in Council appointed on July 4, 1660, a committee, known as "The Right Honorable the Lords appointed a Committee of this Board for Trade and Plantations." The members were Edward Montague, Earl of Manchester, the Lord Chamberlain; Thomas Wriothesley, Earl of Southampton, the Lord Treasurer; Robert Sydney, Earl of Leicester; William Fiennes, Lord Say and Seale; John Lord Robartes; Denzil

Holles, Arthur Annesley, Sir Anthony Ashley Cooper, and the Secretaries of State, Sir Edward Nicholas and Sir William Morrice. The committee was instructed to meet on every Monday and Thursday at three o'clock in the afternoon, "to review, heare, examine, and deliberate upon any petitions, propositions, memorials, or other addresses, which shall be presented or brought in by any person or persons concerning the plantations, as well in the Continent as Islands of America, and from time to time make their report to this board of their proceedings."[85]

Work of Privy Council Committee

It is evident from the wording of these instructions that the committee was designed to be a continuous one and to carry on the work of the former committee for foreign plantations of the Council of State. There is no essential difference between these committees, except that one represented a commonwealth and the other a monarchy. We pass from the one arrangement to the other with very little jar, and with much less sense of a break in the continuity than when we pass from the system under the Republic to that under the Protectorate. The Privy Council committee had all the essential features of a standing committee and, after the experiment with separate and select councils had proved unsatisfactory, it assumed entire control of trade and plantation affairs in 1675, a control which it exercised until 1696. Though an occasional change was made in its membership and some reorganization was effected in 1668, the Lords of Trade of July 4, 1660, commissioned with plenary powers by patent under the great seal, became the Lords of Trade of February 9, 1675.

From 1660 to 1675 this committee of the Privy Council played no insignificant part although, after the creation of the councils, it was bound to be limited in the actual work that it performed. During the four months after its appointment it was the only body that had to do with trade and plantations except the Privy Council, which occasionally sat as a committee of the whole for plantation affairs. During the summer the committee considered with care and a due regard for all aspects of the case the claims of various persons to the government of Barbadoes. Despite the opposition of Modyford, who had been commissioned governor by the Council of State the April before, and John Colleton, one of the Council of Barbadoes, and despite the efforts of Alderman Riccard and other merchants of London, Francis Lord Willoughby was restored to the government under the claims of the Earl of Carlisle. At the same time the claims of the Kirks, Elliott, and Sterling to Nova Scotia were examined and eventually decided in favor of Col. Temple, the governor there. Willoughby immediately appointed Capt. Watts governor of the Caribbee Islands, himself, through his deputy, took the governorship of Barbadoes, Modyford became governor of Jamaica, Berkeley of Virginia, and Russell of Nevis. It is at least worthy of recall that Willoughby, Watts, Temple, and Russell were all within the circle of Povey's friends, that Povey and Noell both petitioned the King for Russell's reappointment, and that Temple wrote Povey begging him to exert his influence in his (Temple's) behalf, lest he lose the governorship. Povey was certainly in high favor with the monarchy; in 1660 he was appointed trea-

---

[85] Cal. State Papers, Col., 1514–1660, pp. 482, 483; P.C.R., Charles II, Vol. II, p. 63; New York Colonial Docts., III, p. 30.

surer to the Duke of York and Master of Requests to his Majesty in Extraordinary June 22, 1660,[86] and during the years that followed he held office after office and with all the skill of a politician continued to find offices for his kinsmen. William Blathwayt, of later fame, was his nephew. Noell was no less honored; he became a member of the Royal Company of Merchants, the Royal African Company, the Society for the Propagation of the Gospel in New England, and was finally knighted in 1663 and died in 1665.[87] As we shall see, both men became very active in the affairs of the plantations, and it is more than likely that the opinions of the King in Council were not infrequently shaped by their suggestions and advice.

Appointment of Select Councils of Trade and Plantations, 1660

How early the decision was reached to create separate councils of trade and foreign plantations it is impossible to say. Some time between May and August, 1660, Povey must have planned to recast his "Overtures" and to present them for the consideration of the King. At first he endeavored to adapt those of 1657 to the new situation by substituting "Foreign Plantations" for the "West Indies," "Matie" for "Highness," and "his Maties Privie Councill" for "the great Councill"; but he finally decided to present a new draft, in which, however, he retained many of the essential clauses of the former paper. Whether the recommendations of Povey as presented in the "Overtures" influenced Lord Clarendon to recommend such councils to the King we cannot say; it is more likely that the practice adopted under the Protectorate had already commended itself to the Chancellor, who was beginning to show that interest in the plantations which characterizes the early years of his administration. That he should have consulted Noell and Povey and other London merchants is to be expected of the man who for at least five years kept up a close correspondence with Maverick of New England, Ludwell of Virginia, and D'Oyley, Littleton, and Modyford in the West Indies,[88] and who was constantly urging upon the King the importance of the plantations as sources of revenue and the great financial possibilities that lay in the improvement of trade. On August 17, 1660, the King in Council drafted a letter to "Our very good Lord the Lord Maior of the Citty of London & to the Court of Aldermen of the said City," reading as follows:

> "After our hearty commendations these are to acquaint you, That his Majesty having this day taken into his princely consideration how necessary it is for the good of this kingdom, that Trade and Commerce with foreign parts, be with all due care, incouraged and maintayned, And for the better settling thereof declared

[86] P.C.R., Charles II, Vol. II, p. 37; Bodleian, Rawlinson A., 117, No. 20.

[87] Professor Osgood thinks that a part of Noell's fortune was made in the slave trade. Beyond the fact that he was a member of the Royal African Company, I cannot find any evidence whatever to prove this statement. Noell certainly was not a slave trader before 1660.

[88] Bodleian, Clarendon Papers, *passim*, New York Hist. Soc. Collections, 1869; Brit. Museum, Add. MSS., 11410, ff. 18 et seq. Clarendon had an agent in Jamaica, Major Ivy, who was considering the setting up of plantations and planting cocoa walks in the interest of the King's revenue. Clarendon's policy toward the continental colonies overshadows somewhat his policy toward the West Indies and in consequence this phase of the subject has been neglected by those who have dealt with Clarendon's colonial relations.

his gracious intention to appoint a Committee of understanding able persons, to take into their particular consideration all things conducible thereunto; We do by his Ma^{ts} special command and in order to the better carrying on of this truly royal, profitable, and advantageous designe, desire you to give notice hereof unto the Turkey Merchants, the Merchant Adventurers, the East India, Greenland, and Eastland Companys, and likewise to the unincorporated Traders, for Spain, France, Portugal, Italy, and the West India Plantations; Willing them out of their respective societies to present unto his Majesty the names of fower of their most knowing active men (of whom, when his Majesty shall have chosen two and unto this number of merchants added some other able and well experienced persons, dignified also with the presence and assistance of some of his Majesty's Privy Council) All those to be by his Matie appointed constituted and authoried by commission under the Great Seal as a Standing Committee, to enquire into and rectify all things tending to the Advancement of Trade and Commerce; That so by their prudent and faithful council and advice, his Matie may (now in this conjuncture, whilst most Foraigne Princes and Potentates doe, upon his Maties most happy establishment upon his throne, seek to renew their former Allyances with this Crowne), insert into the several Treatyes, such Articles & Clauses as may render this Nation more prosperous and flourishing in Trade and Commerce. Thus by prudence, care, & industry improving those great advantages to the highest point of felicity, which by its admirable situation Nature seems to have indulged to this his Majesty's kingdom. So we bid you heartily farewell."[89]

Membership of these Councils

This letter was signed by Chancellor Hyde, Earl of Southampton, George Monck, Earl of Albemarle, Lord Say and Seale, Earl of Manchester, Lord Robartes, Arthur Annesley, and Secretary Morrice, who probably formed a special committee appointed to draft it. Some time within the month the answer of the Aldermen must have been received, for on September 19 the Council ordered the attorney general "to make a draught of a commission for establishing a Councell of Trade according to the grounds layed" in the letter of the seventeenth of August, "upon the perusal whereof at the Board his Matie will insert the names of the said Counsell." It is more than likely that the project for the second council, that of plantations, went forward *pari passu* with the Council for Trade and that the letter to the

---

[89] P.C.R., Charles II, Vol. II, pp. 131–132; printed in part in Analytical Index to the Series of Records known as the Remembrancia, preserved among the Archives of the City of London, 1579–1664. (Privately printed, 1878); and in very much abbreviated form in Bannister, Writings of William Patterson, III, 251–252, from whom it has been copied by both Egerton and Cunningham. It seems somewhat strange that there should be no entry of the receipt of this letter in the journal of the court of Aldermen nor any draft of an answer among the Remembrancia or elsewhere. A careful search has failed to disclose any reference to action taken upon this letter among the papers in the Town Clerk's office at the Guildhall.

Mayor and Aldermen served a double purpose. At any rate that must have been the understanding among those interested at the time, for on September 26, one Norwich, Captain of the Guards, who had been in Clarendon's employ, sent in a memorial to the Chancellor begging that the King employ him "in his customs and committees of trade and forraign plantations."[90] The matter of drafting the commissions must have taken some time, for they are not mentioned as ready for the addition of names before the last week in October. The business of making up the lists of members must have been a difficult and tedious matter. Many lists exist among the Domestic Papers which contain changes, erasures and additions, drafts and corrected drafts, which show how much pains Clarendon and the others took to make the membership of the Council of Trade satisfactory. A suggested list was first drawn up containing the names of privy councillors, country gentlemen, customers, merchants, traders, the navy officers, gentlemen versed in affairs, and doctors of civil law. With this list was considered another containing the names of the persons nominated by the different merchant companies. Other lists seem also to have been presented.[91] Probably in much the same way the list of the members of the Council for Foreign Plantations was made up, but more slowly.

The commissions were both ready by October 25 and on November 7 had reached the Crown Office (Chancery), ready to pass the great seal. The commission for the Council of Trade passed the great seal on that day and is dated November 7, 1660; but the commission for the Council for Foreign Plantations was held back that the names of other members might be added and it became necessary to have a new bill passed and duly engrossed three weeks later.[92] Therefore the commission for the Council for Foreign Plantations is dated December 1, 1660.

An analysis of the membership of these two councils and of the membership of the Royal African Company, created soon after, shows many points of interest. The Council of Trade consisted of sixty-two members, that of Foreign Plantations of forty-eight,[93] and that of the African Company of sixty-six. Twenty-eight members are common to the first two bodies, eleven are common to the Council of Trade and the Royal African Company, and eight are common to all three groups. These eight are John Lord Berkeley of Stratton; Sir George Carteret, Sir Nicholas Crispe, Sir Andrew Riccard, Sir John Shaw, Thomas Povey, Martin Noell, and John Colleton. The other members common to the two councils are Lord Clarendon, the Earl of Southampton, Earl of Manchester, Earl of Marlborough, Earl of Portland, Lord Robartes, Francis Lord Willoughby, Denzil Holles, Sir Edward Nicholas, Sir William Morrice, Arthur Annesley, Sir Anthony Ashley Cooper, William Coventry, Daniel O'Neale, Sir James Draxe, Edward Waller, Edward Digges, William Williams, Thomas Kendall, and John Lewis; while among the other members of

[90] Bodleian, Clarendon Papers, 73, f. 232.
[91] Cal. State Papers, Dom., 1660–1661, p. 319.
[92] Public Record Office, Chancery, Crown Dockets, 6, p. 50. On the docket for the commission of the council of trade the names of the members are inserted; but on that of the commission for the council for foreign plantations the place is left blank. A marginal note on the latter docket gives the explanation noted above.
[93] There is a list of the members in 1661, containing but forty-seven names with some omissions and additions.

the Council for Foreign Plantations are such well-known men as Sir William Berkeley, Capt. John Limbrey, Col. Edward Waldrond, Capt. Thomas Middleton, Capt. William Watts, and Capt. Alexander Howe. Thus the merchants, sea-captains, and planters, men thoroughly familiar with the questions of trade and plantations and intimately connected with the plantations themselves are members of the Council of Plantations and sometimes of that of Trade also. It is significant that among the four London merchants common to all three groups should be found the names of Noell and Povey. Their associates, Crispe and Riccard, were persons well known in the history of London trade, and probably the four names represent the four most influential men among the merchants of London who supported the King. When we turn to the work of these councils we shall see that Povey and Noell were active members also.

Comparison of Povey's "Overtures" with the Instructions for Council for Foreign Plantations

However uncertain we may be regarding the influence of Povey and Noell in shaping the policy of Clarendon and the King, that uncertainty disappears as soon as we examine the instructions which were drafted to accompany the commission for a Council for Foreign Plantations. The instructions are little more than a verbal reproduction of the "Overtures" which Povey drafted some time during the summer of 1660 for presentation to the King. They are based on the earlier overtures and proposals and certain passages can be traced back unchanged to the first "Overture" of 1654. Seven of the eleven clauses are taken from the Povey papers as follows:

Overtures.	*Instructions.*
They may forthwith write letters to everie Governour ... requiring an exact and perticular Account of the State of their affairs; of the nature and constitution of their Lawes and Government, and in what modell they move; what numbers of them, what Fortifications, and other Strengths, and Defences are upon the Places.	2. You shall forthwith write letters to evrie of our Governo^rs ... to send unto 3. you ... perticular and exact accompt of the state of their affaires; of the nature and constitution of their lawes and governm^t and in what modell and frame they move and are disposed; what numbers of men; what fortifications and other strengths and defences are upon the place.
To apply to all prudentiall meanes for the rendering these Dominions usefull to England, and England helpfull to them; and that the Severall Pieces, and Collonies bee drawn and disposed into a more certaine, civill, and uniform waie of Government; and distribution of publick justice.	5. To applie your selves to all prudentiall means for the rendering those dominions usefull to England, and England helpful to them, and for the bringing the severall Colonies and Plantacons, within themselves, into a more certaine civill and uniforme [waie] of government and for the better ordering and distributeing of publicque justice among them.

To settle such a continuall correspondencie, that it may be able to give upp an account once a yeare to his Matie of the Goverment of each Place; of their Complaints, their Wants, their Aboundance, of everie Shipp trading there, and its lading; and whither consign'd; and to know what the proceeds of that Place have been that yeare; whereby the instrinsick value, and the true condition of each part and of the whole may be thoroughly understood; and whereby a Ballance may be erected for the better ordering and disposing of Trade, and of the growth of the Plantations, that soe, each Place within itself and all of them being as it were made up into one Comonwealth, may by his Matie bee heere governd, and regulated accordingly, upon common and equal principles.

To enquire diligently into the Severall Governments and Councells of Plantations belonging to forreigne Princes, or States; and examine by what Conduct and Pollicies they govern, or benefitt their own Collonies, and upon what Grounds. And is to consult and provide soe, that if such Councells be good, wholesome, and practicable, they may be applyed to our use; or if they tend, or were designed to our prejudice or Disadvantage, they may bee ballanced, or turned-back upon them.

To receive, debate, and favour all such Propositions as shall be tendered to them, for the improvement of any of the forreigne Plantations, or in order to any other laudable and advantageous enterprize.

4. To order and settle such a continuall correspondencie that you may be able, as often as you are required thereunto, to give up to us an accompt of the Governm^t of each Colonie; of their complaints, their wants, their abundance; of their severall growths and comodities of every Shipp Tradeing there and its ladeing and whither consigned and what the proceeds of that place have beene in the late years; that thereby the intrinsick value and the true condicon of each part of the whole may be thoroughly understood; whereby a more steady judgem^t and ballance may be made for the better ordering and disposing of trade & of the proceede and improvem^ts of the Plantacons; that soe each place within it selfe, and all of them being collected into one viewe and managem^t here, may be regulated and ordered upon common and equall ground & principles.

6. To enquire diligently into the severall governm^ts and Councells of Colonies Plantacons and distant Dominions, belonging to other Princes or States, and to examine by what conduct and pollicies they govern or benefit them; and you are to consult and provide that if such councells be good wholesome and practicable, they may be applied to the case of our Plantacons; or if they tend or were designed to the prejudice or disadvantage thereof or of any of our subjects or of trade or comerce, how then they may be ballanced or turned back upon them.

11. To advise, order, settle, and dispose of all matters relating to the good governm^t improvement and management of our Forraine Plantacons or any of them, with your utmost skill direccon and prudence.

To call to its Advice and Consultation from time to time, as often as the matter in debate and under consideration shall require, any well experienced Persons, whether Mechants, or Seamen, or Artificers.

7. To call to your assistance from time to time as often as the matter in consideration shall require any well experienced persons, whether merchants, planters, seamen, artificers, etc.

In the "Overtures" there are no clauses corresponding to those in the Instructions relating to the enforcement of the Navigation Act or to the spread of the Christian religion; these may well be deemed Restoration additions, inserted at Clarendon's request. But the clause concerning the transportation of servants, poor men, and vagrants may well have been Povey's own, for both Povey and Noell were interested in the question and Noell had been in the business since 1654. In the "Queries" is the following paragraph:

> "Whither the weeding of this Comon Wealth of Vagabonds, condemned Persons and such as are heere useless and hurtful in wars and peace, and a settled course taken for the transporting them to the Indias and thereby principally supplying Jamaica is not necessary to be consulted."

Among the Povey papers is one entitled "Certain propositions for the better accommodating the Forreigne Plantacons with Servants," which Povey may have drawn up. Hence, there is no good reason to doubt but that Povey wrote the entire draft of these instructions himself. Even those portions that are not to be found in the "Overtures" are written in Povey's peculiar and rather stilted style.

Comparison of Povey's "First Draft" with Instructions for Council of Trade

That Povey and Noell were the authors of the instructions given to the Council of Trade it is not so easy to demonstrate. A preliminary sketch of "Instructions for a Councill of Trade" as well as a copy of the final instructions are to be found among the Povey papers and both Povey and Noell were sufficiently familiar with the requirements of trade at that period to have drafted such a document. The fact that the second paper is but an elaboration of the first leads to the conclusion that they bear to each other much the same relation that the "Overtures" bear to the Instructions for the Council of Plantations:

FIRST DRAFT.

1. You shall in the first place consider, and propound how to remedy inconveniencys of the the English trade, in all the respective dominions of those Princes and States with whom his Mat^{ie} may renew Alliance, and to that end make due enquiry into such former treaties as relate to Trade.

FINAL INSTRUCTIONS.

1. You shall take into your consideration the inconveniences wch the English Trade hath suffered in any Partes beyond the Seas, And are to inquire into such Articles of former Treaties as have been made with any Princes or States in relation to Trade, And to draw out such Observations or Resolutions from thence, as may be necessary for us to advise or insist upon in any

What Articles have bin provided in favour of the Trade of his Maties Subjects, How they have been neglected & Violated, What new Capitulations may be necessary pro Ratione Rerum, et temporum.

And those, either in Relation:

1. To the freedome of Sale of your Commodities of all sorts, as to price & payment.

2. To the best expedition of Justice for recovery of your debts.

3. To the security of the Estates of all factors, and their Principalls in case of the factor's death.

4. To the Prevention of the Interruption of the Trade & Navigation, by Embargos of forraigne Princes & States, or impresinge your Shipps to their Service.

5. To the Interest of all Trades that are or shall be incorporated by his Mat^ies Charters, what jurisdictyon is necessary to be obtained from our Allies, for the more regular government of the Trade & members of those Corporations in forraigne factoryes.

2^ly. And next you shall consider, how the reputation of all the manufactures of his Mat^ies Kingdome may be recovered by a just regulation and standard of weight, length, and breadth, that soe the more profitable and ample Vent of them may be procured.

forreigne Leagues or Allyances. That such evills as have befallen these our Kingdomes through the want of good information in these great and publique concernm^ts may be provided against in tyme to come.

2. You are to consider how & by whome any former Articles or Treatyes have been neglected or violated, what new Capitulations are necessary either to the freedome of Sale of your Commodities of all sorts, as to price & payment, Or to the best expedition of Justice to the recovery of Debts, or to the Security of Estates of all factors & their Principalls in case of the factor's Death, Or to the prevention of those interruptions wch the Trade & Navigations of our Kingdomes have suffered by Imbargoes of forreigne Princes or States, Or Impresinge the Shipps of any of our Subjects, for their Service.

3. You are to consider well the Interest of all such trades as are or shall be Incorporated by our Royall Charters, & what Jurisdictions are necessary to be obteyned from such as are, or shall be in Allyance with us, for the more regular managem^t & governm^t of the Trade, & of the members of those our Corporations & forreigne factories.

4. You are to consider of the severall Manufactures of these our Kingdomes how & by what occasions they are corrupted, debased & disparaged, And by what probable meanes they may be restored & maintained in their auncyent goodness & reputation, And how they may be farther improved to there utmost advantage by a just Regulation & Standard of weight Length & Breadth, that soe the private profitt of the Tradesmen or Merchants may not destroy the Creditt of the Commodity,

& thereby render it neglected & unvended abroad, to the great loss & scandall of these our Kingdomes.

5. You are also to take into your Consideration all the native Commodities of the growth & production of these our Kingdomes, and how they may be ordered, nourished, increased & manifactured to the ymployment of our People and to the best advantage of the Publique.

4^ly. How the fishinge Trades of Newfound Land, the Coasts of England, Irland, & New England may be most improoved, and regulated to the greatest advantage of the Stocke and navigation of the nation, by excludinge the intrusion of our neighbors into it.

6. You are especially to consider of the whole business of fishings of these our Kingdomes or any other of our distant Dominions or Plantations & to consult of some effectuall meanes for the reinforceing encouraging & encreasinge, and for the regulating & carryinge on of the Trade in all the Parts thereof. To the end That the People and Stock, and Navigation of these our Kingdomes may be ymployed therein and our Neighbors may not be enricht with that which soe properly & advantagiously may be undertooke & carryed on by our own Subjects.

3^ly. How the Trade of the Kingdome to forraigne parts may be soe menaged and proportioned, that we may in every part be more Sellers than buyers, that thereby the Coyne and present Stocke of money may be preserved and increased.

7. You are seriously to consider & enquire whether the Importation of forreigne Commodityes doe not over-ballance the Exportations of such as are Native, And how it may be soe Ordered remedied, & proportioned that we may have more Sellers than Buyers in every parte abroad, And that the Coyne & present Stock of these our Kingdomes, may be preserved & increased, We judging, that such a Scale & Rule of proportion is one of the highest and most prudentiall points of Trade by wch the riches & strength of these our Kingdomes, are best to be understood & maintained.

8. You are to consider & examine by what wayes & means other Nations doe preferr their owne growths & Manifactures, & Importations, & doe discourage & suppress those of these our Kingdomes, & how the best contrivances and managem^t of Trade, exercysed by other Nations may be rendred applicable & practicable by these our Kingdomes.

9. You are well to consider all matters relatinge to Navigation, & to the increase, & the Security thereof.

10. You are thoroughly to consider the severall matters relatinge to Money, how Bullonge may be best drawne in hither, & how any Obstructions upon our Mynt may be best removed.

5^{ly}. How the forraigne Plantations may be made most useful to the Trade & Navigation of these Kingdomes.

11. You are to consider the generall State & Condition of our forreigne Plantations & of the Navigation Trade & severall Commodityes ariseinge thereupon, & how farr theire future Improvem^t & Prosperitie may bee advanced by any discouragement Imposition or Restraint, upon the Importation of all goods or Commodityes wth which those Plantations doe abound, and may supply these our Kingdomes, And you are alsoe in all matters wherein our forreigne Plantations are concerned to take advise or information (as occasion shall require) from the Councell appointed & sett apart by us to the more perticuler Inspection Regulation and Care of our forreigne plantations.

12. You are to consider how the transportation of such things may be best restreined and prevented, as are either forbidden by the Lawe, or may be inconvenient, or of disadvantage by being transported out of these our Kingdomes and dominions.[94]

---

[94] Egerton, 2395, ff. 268, 269; Cal. State Papers, Dom., 1660–1661, pp. 353–354; P.R.O.

Work of Council for Foreign Plantations, 1660–1665

The councils thus commissioned and instructed soon met for organization and business, the Council for Plantations holding its preliminary session December 10, 1660, in the Star Chamber, and all remaining meetings in the Inner Court of Wards; the Council for Trade meeting, first, in Mercer's Hall, near Old Jewry, afterwards in certain rooms in Whitehall, still later in a rented house which was consumed in the great fire, and, after 1667, in Exeter House, Strand. Philip Frowde became the clerical secretary of the Plantation Council and George Duke secretary of the Council of Trade, a position that he seems to have lost in 1663 but to have resumed again before 1667. The meetings were attended chiefly by the non-conciliar members, for it was usually the rule that privy councillors were to be present only when some special business required their coöperation. Both councils were organized in much the same manner, with a number, at least seven, of inferior officers, clerks, messengers, and servants, and in both cases journals of proceedings and entry books containing copies of documents, patents, charters, petitions, and reports were kept.[95] Whether minutes were taken of the meetings of the subcommittees is

---

State Papers, Domestic, XXI, No. 27; Cunningham, Growth of English Industry and Commerce, 4 ed., Appendix.

[95] The journal of the Council of Plantations is among the Colonial Papers in the Public Record Office, XIV, No. 59, ff. 1–57, December 1, 1660–August 4, 1664, entitled "Orders and Proceedings at his Ma^ts Counsell for Forraigne Plantacons." There is no journal of the Council of Trade known to exist, but minutes of one or two meetings, which have been preserved, show that a journal must have been kept. An entry-book for patents is mentioned, Cal. State Papers, Col., 1661–1668, § 15, and an entry-book of petitions and reports, November 13, 1660–March 12, 1662, is in Brit. Mus. Add. MSS., 25115.

Regarding the history of the papers of the Council of Trade the following information may be of interest. The records probably remained in the possession of George Duke, secretary to the Council, and were called for by Dr. Worsley, secretary of the Council of 1672 in a letter dated November 28, 1672 (Cal. State Papers, Dom., 1672–1673, pp. 213–214). No answer was received from Duke and evidently the papers were not handed over, for when in 1698 the Board of Trade applied for them to Col. Duke's son-in-law, Henry Crispe, it was informed by Mr. Crispe that he had never even seen any of the papers but had heard that some of them were burnt in the Temple when in Col. Duke's possession (Journal of the Board of Trade, XI, p. 55, May 10, 1698). In June and July, 1707, the Board of Trade attempted again to get hold of the papers and wrote to Crispe on June 30. Crispe's reply is worth printing:

"If I am rightly informed there are divers original books and papers relating to the Royal Fishery and the establishing thereof from the year 1660 for divers successive years in which are contained several projections concerning the promoting the same. And there are also books and minutes of the proceedings of the Council of Trade from the year 1660 to 1668, which also contain several material things in relation to Trade and the improvement thereof, which I understand are in the power of a friend of mine.

"These books and papers will be disposed of as the Honble Board the Council of Trade shall direct or order.

"But it is humbly desired that consideration be allowed the party that shall produce these Books and Papers. And that it may be ascertained what that consideration shall be and by whom it shall be given.

doubtful; no such papers have anywhere been found.

The Council for Plantations had a continuous existence from December 10, 1660, when the preliminary meeting was held, probably until the spring of 1665, though August 24, 1664, is the date of its last recorded sitting. During that time it shared in the extraordinary activity which characterized the early years of the Restoration and represents, as far as such activity can represent any one person, the enthusiasm of the Earl of Clarendon. There was not an important phase of colonial life and government, not a colonial claim or dispute, that was not considered carefully, thoroughly, and, in the main, impartially by the Council.[96] The business was nearly always handled, in the first instance, by experts, for with few exceptions the working committees were made up of men who had had intimate experience with colonial affairs or were financially interested in their prosperity. The first committee, that of January 7, 1661, for example, was composed of Sir Anthony Ashley Cooper, who had been on plantation committees during the Interregnum; Robert Boyle, president of the Corporation for the Propagation of the Gospel in New England and one of the founders of the Royal Society; Sir Peter Leere and Sir James Draxe, old Barbadian planters; Edmund Waller, poet and parliamentarian, who had been interested in colonial affairs for some years; General Venables, who knew Jamaica well; Thomas Povey, Edward Digges, John Colleton (soon to be Sir John), Martin Noell (soon to be Sir Martin), and Thomas Kendall, all merchants and experts on colonial trade, and Middleton, Jefferies, Watts, and Howe, sea-captains and merchants in frequent touch with the colonies. Other committees were made up in much the same way, although the number of members was usually smaller. When letters were to be written or reports drafted that required skill in composition and embodiment in literary form, we find the task entrusted to Povey alone or to Povey assisted by the poets Waller and Sir John Denham. Povey was, indeed, the most active member of the Council, serving as its secretary in much the same capacity as on the Committee for America from 1657 to 1660.[97] On both these boards he exemplified his own recommendation that there should be on

"I was desired to inform you of this to the end you may take such steps therein as you in your great prudence shall judge most proper.

"If any orders or commands shall be given about this affair that I can be useful or serviceable therein & they be transmitted for me or be left at Johns Coffee House in Bedford St. near the Church in Convent Garden such orders will be faithfully observed by

"Srs Your faithfull humble Servant
"H. Crispe."

Crispe sent a list of the books with his letter, but that list is missing. The Board answered that it would not buy the books without seeing them first, but as we find no further mention of the matter in the Journal and as the books and papers are not to be found to-day the probabilities are that the negotiations fell through. Journal, XIX, p. 296; Board of Trade Papers, Trade, H Nos. 74, 76.

[96] This may be inferred from the following note attached to one of the reports: "The council conceiving themselves to be in noe capacitie of giving any judgment therein having heard but one side." Egerton, 2395, f. 299.

[97] See Cal. State Papers, Col., 1675–1676, §§ 338, 339, where he is called "Secretary for Foreign Plantations."

the Council "a Person who is to be more imediately concern'd and active than the rest ... allwaies readie to give a full and digested account and consideracon of any particular relating to those Affaires." Among the Povey papers are many drafts of letters and reports in process of construction, bearing erasures and additions which point to Povey as their author.[98]

The Council for Plantations and its committees sat and deliberated apart, the latter in Grocer's Hall; but the subjects under examination were considered by both bodies. The subcommittees were frequently instructed to call in persons interested, to write to others from whom information could be obtained, and to pursue their investigations with due regard for both sides of the case. Sometimes questions would be submitted to the attorney general, to Dr. Walter Walker and others from Doctors Commons, to special members of the Council who were more familiar than the rest with the facts in the case. On at least one occasion all the members of the Council were requested to bring in what information they could obtain regarding a particular matter. Question after question was postponed from one meeting to another, because the Council had not obtained all the details that it felt should be in hand before the report was sent to the King in Council. On a few occasions members of the Council accompanied the report to the Privy Council apparently with the intention of explaining or emphasizing their recommendations. The subjects under debate concerned the internal or external affairs of all the colonies. They related to Jamaica, Barbadoes, Maryland, Virginia, and New England, including Nova Scotia, Massachusetts, Maine, and Long Island; they dealt with Quakers, Jews, vagrants, and servants, supplies, provisions, naval stores, emigrant registration, and abuses in colonial trade; they included that burning question of the period, the Dutch at New Amsterdam and the complaints that arose regarding Holland as an obstruction to English trade. The amount of time taken and pains expended on controversial points can be inferred from an examination of the New England case, which was taken up at the first regular meeting in January and was under examination from that time until April 30, when the Council sent in its report. Even then it was taken up by the Privy Council, referred to its own committee, called the Committee for New England, and in one or two particulars was sent back to the Council for further consideration. In the performance of its duties the Council for Plantations can never be charged with indolence or neglect. In the year 1661 alone it held forty meetings, or an average of one every nine days.

After August, 1664, the records of the Council come to an end, but there is reason to believe that the Council continued its sessions at least until the spring of 1665. That the last meeting was not held on August 24 is certain, not only from the wording of the minute, which reads: "ordered, being a matter of great moment and the day far spent, that the further consideration be deferred for a week," but also from two further references to the existence of the Council, of later date, — one dated September 7, when the Council sent in a report regarding the proposed establishment of a registry office, and the other in the form of an endorsement upon a letter from Lord Willoughby which says: "Ref^d to the Council, Feb. 24," that is February 24, 1665. It seems probable, therefore, that the Council was sitting as

---

[98] Egerton, 2395, ff. 286, 291, 299, 335, 336.

late as February-March of that year.[99] Probably its meetings were broken up by the plague which started in London about that time, in the westernmost parish, St. Giles-in-the-Fields, and lasted until the end of October. Whether the Council resumed its sessions after the plague had subsided it is almost impossible to say. No definite record exists of its meetings or work. Some of its members had died, Sir Martin Noell in October, 1665, and Sir Nicholas Crispe the next year; others had left England, Lord Willoughby, Capts. Watts and Kendall, and possibly Sir James Draxe; while others had accepted posts that took them away from London, as in the case of Capt. Middleton, who became commissioner of the navy at Portsmouth. Certainly Povey could have had very little to do with the affairs of a council in London in 1664–1666, when as surveyor-general of the victualling department he was required to be frequently at Plymouth and to spend a considerable amount of time travelling about England.[100] Yet there is nothing to show that its commission was revoked, and an order of the Privy Council, September 23, 1667, to which further reference will be made below, reads as if the Council were in existence at that time. If so, it must have been merely a nominal body.

Control of Plantation Affairs, 1665–1670

After 1665, and until 1670, plantation affairs seem to have been controlled entirely by the Privy Council and its committees, which proved themselves capable and vigorous bodies. Before 1666, besides the Committee for Foreign Plantations, which has already been noticed, other committees were appointed as occasion arose, — committees for Jamaica, for Jamaica and Algiers, for the Guinea trade, for the Royal Company, for fishing in Newfoundland, for Jersey and Guernsey, and for New England. Committees for Trade and for hearing appeals from the Plantations also existed. On December 7, 1666, after the plague had subsided and the great fire had spent itself, the Privy Council reappointed its plantation committee, which now entered upon a career of greatly increased activity.[101] At the same time the Council made use of its other committees, particularly the "Committee for the Affaires of New England and for the bounding of Acadia," October 2, 4, 1667, which took into consideration the question of the restitution of Acadia to the French;[102] and it referred important matters of business to committees of selected experts. Under these conditions the affairs of the colonies were managed until the appointment of a new Plantation Council in August, 1670.

Work of Council of Trade, 1660–1664

The Council for Trade met in Mercer's Hall some time before November 13, 1660, and at its preliminary session considered that part of its instructions which related to bullion and coin. On December 13, 1660, it passed a resolution urging and inviting people and merchants to send in petitions, and it requested the King

---

[99] Cal. State Papers, Col., 1661–1668, §§ 790, 833; Dom., 1664–1665, p. 4.

[100] In December, 1665, he wrote of "an uncomfortable journey on unfrequented roads, with none to break the ice, in a hackney coach which receives the wind in all parts." Cal. State Papers, Dom., 1665, p. 105.

[101] P.C.R., Charles II, Vol. VI, p. 231; Cal. State Papers, Col., 1661–1668, § 1685.

[102] Egerton, 2395, ff. 449, 451, 452, 453; Cal. State Papers, Col., 1661–1668, §§ 1598–1600.

to issue a proclamation defining its powers in all matters relating to trade and manufactures and calling on "any person, concerned in the matters therein to be debated or who have any petition or invention to offer, to apply to them for redress of evils brought on by the late times or for the improvement of trade regulations."[103] In response to, this appeal a large number of petitions, sent either to the Privy Council or directly to the Select Council itself, were received, and the discussion of these petitions and the preparing of reports upon them occupied the attention of the Council during the first two years. These reports show that the Council took its duties seriously and was thoroughly in earnest to improve, if possible, the trade of the kingdom, and to carry out to the full the commands which the King had laid upon it. There is not a clause of the instructions to which it did not pay some attention, and upon many matters it debated long and ardently, making reports that are as valuable for the student of the trade policy of the seventeenth century as are the familiar writings of well-known mercantilists. The Council took up and discussed the export of bullion and coin, expressing its opinion that the penalties should be withdrawn as injurious to trade, because they prevented the English merchants from bringing their money into the kingdom where it would be detained, and saying that money most abounded in countries which enjoyed freedom from restraints on exports. The trade in the Baltic, the East Indies, and the Levant to which trade freedom to export bullion was preeminently important; the Merchant Adventurers, regarding whose history and position the Council made a valuable report, viewing the subject from the beginning; the East India Company, whose petition,—largely reproduced in the report of the Council,—contained a bitter arraignment of the Dutch, calling to mind the "impudent affronts to the honor of this nation and the horrid injuries done to the stock and commerce thereof," and demanding damages and a definite regulation of trade in the forthcoming treaty with Holland then under debate; treaties with foreign powers, clauses in which concerning trade were taken up at the early meetings of the Council; prohibition of imposts on foreign cloths and stuffs, regarding which sundry shopkeepers, tradesmen, and artificers of London had petitioned the Privy Council in November, 1660,[104]—all these matters the Council took under consideration. It dealt with the granting of patents, with the encouragement of home industries, particularly the business of the framework knitters, silk-dyeing, and the manufacture of tapestry, and with the establishment of an insurance company.[105] As far as the plantations were concerned, its recommendations were few, and were made chiefly in connection with reports on the ninth and eleventh articles of its instructions, which touched upon convoys, imports, and composition-ports. It drafted a carefully drawn list of necessary convoys in which, of all the American plantations, only Newfoundland is mentioned. It considered the importation of logwood and tobacco, and upon the latter point made the suggestion "that all tobacco of English Plantations do pay at importation ½d. a pound and at exportation

[103] Brit. Mus., Add. MSS., 25115, f. 156; Cal. State Papers, Dom., 1661–1662, pp. 411–412.

[104] Brit. Mus., Add. MSS., 25115; Cal. State Papers, Dom., 1660–1661, pp. 356, 359, 363, 372, 412; 1661–1662 pp. 28, 80.

[105] Cal. State Papers, Dom., 1660–1661, pp. 383, 532; 1661–1662, pp. 111, 277, 529, 446; Bodleian, Rawlinson MSS., A. 478, f. 81.

nothing." This recommendation was accompanied by a valuable essay on trade in general. It dealt with the question of making Dover a free port for composition trade and took the ground that the Acts of Navigation should be inviolably kept. On this question the Earl of Southampton, the Treasurer, and Lord Ashley (Cooper), Chancellor of the Exchequer, took the opposite ground, favoring the freedom of the port, "Dover having formerly been a port for free trade," and adding that "a free trade thus settled we conceive might conduce to the advantage of your Majesty's customs," trade being injured by the "tyes and observances which the Act of Navigation places upon it." They reported further that the farmers of the customs wished the Act to be dispensed with in some cases.[106]

Regarding the attitude of the Council toward the sixth article of its instructions, the promotion of the fisheries, we have fuller information. At the session of December 17, 1663, there were present the Earl of Sandwich, William Coventry, Sir Nicholas Crispe, Henry Slingsby, Christopher Boone, John Lord Berkeley, Sir Sackville Crowe, Thomas Povey, John Jolliffe, and George Toriano. Acting on a special order from the King, they debated how best the fishing trade might be gained and promoted, and how encouraged and advanced when gained. They considered the respective merits of a commission and a corporation, and whether, if a corporation should be agreed upon, it ought to be universal or exclusive, perpetual or limited, a joint stock or a divided stock, and what immunities and powers should be granted, the character of the persons to be admitted and the number. Taking up each point in turn, the members of the Council first considered "How to gain the Trade of Fishery" and laid down seven methods: 1, 2, by raising money either through voluntary contributions or through lotteries; 3, 4, by restraint of foreign importation or by impositions upon all foreign importation; 5, by letters to all countries urging them to contribute such especial commodities as cordage, lumber, boards, and the like, in exchange for fish; 6, by declaring a war against the Dutch, and at the same time, 7, by naturalizing or indenizing all Hollanders who would come into the English fishery. For the support of the trade when gained the Council proposed: 1, to impose a proportion of fish upon every vintner, innkeeper, alehouse-keeper, victualler, and coffee house in England; 2, to refuse all licenses for fish, which were to be paid for to the corporation; 3, to take the stock of the poor of every parish and provide for the impotent and aged only out of the product, and employ such as were able to work in the fishery—the impotent in the making of nets, etc.; 4, to require the gentlemen of all maritime counties to raise a stock of money in their counties to be employed toward the advance of the fishery; 5, to raise busses, i. e., Dutch herring boats, and to set them forth to their own use and to receive the profits in fish or in the product of it; 6, to employ the imposition laid upon fish by the last Parliament for the purpose of advancing the trade; to accept the offer of fishmongers to raise busses and money; 8, to require the master and wardens of the company, and, 9, to encourage private persons to do the same; 10, to bring over Dutchmen to teach the English the art of curing, salting, and marking fish, and of making casks. It was then decided, "after a long and solemne

[106] Brit. Mus., Add. MSS., 25115, ff. 133–140; Cal. State Papers, Treasury Books, 1660–1667, pp. 245–247, containing the list of convoys, a duplicate of that in the British Museum volume; p. 250, the Treasurer's report.

debate of the whole matter," *nemine contradicente*, "that there being no disadvantage in a corporation But many great Advantages, powers and Immunities that cannot be had by Commission That the best way of advancing & encouraging the Fishing Trade is by way of [a] Corporation." To this corporation were to be granted "the sole power of Lycensing the Eating and killing of flesh in Lent," the power to make by-laws, to dispose of "guifts that are or shalbee given for carrying on of this Trade," to administer oaths, to constitute officers, to exercise coercion in case of contempt against orders, to fine and in some cases to imprison, to send for papers, persons, books, etc. The corporation was to be universal, perpetual, and a joint stock company.[107] As a result of the report of the Council a charter of incorporation was issued to the Duke of York and thirty-six others, forming the Governor and Company of the Royal Fishery of Great Britain and Ireland, and George Duke, "late Secretary to the Committee of Trade," was recommended by the King as its secretary.[108]

This account of the debate in the Council upon the fishery question is important not only because it gives an interesting glimpse of the Council at work, and the only glimpse that we have at any length of its procedure, but because it illustrates a phase of mercantilism in the making. It shows, also, the intensity of the rivalry that existed between England and Holland, and furnishes an admirable example of one of the causes of that rivalry, the Dutch predominance in the fishing business.[109] The Council frequently appealed to the methods employed by the Dutch as a sufficient argument to support its contention, and when objections were raised against the universal corporation it answered, "You destroy the essence of a Corporation by lymitting it, And if you lymitt it, no man will venture their Stocke, and the mayne reason why the Dutch employ not only their Stocke but their whole families in the fisheries, is because their corporation is perpetual."

Parliamentary Committee of Trade, 1664

How much longer the Council of Trade continued its sessions it is impossible to say. Its last recorded action is a report, dated July, 1664, which contained its opinion upon the question of trade with Scotland, a matter soon to be taken up by the higher authorities. It is probable that, as in the case of the Council of Plantations, its sessions were suspended because of the plague and the fire and were not resumed. Its commission was not revoked and it certainly had a nominal existence until 1667. That it had no actual existence in April, 1665, seems likely from a letter sent to the Archbishop of Canterbury at that time, begging that the King appoint a council of trade to find out the cause of the decay in the coal trade.[110] By the summer of 1665 trade was reported dead and money scarce and to the plague was

---

[107] Brit. Mus., Egerton, 2543, ff. 137–139.

[108] Cal. State Papers, Dom., 1663–1664, pp. 515, 549. The Fishing Commission, appointed in 1661, had proved a failure, but the council borrowed from the patent of that commission many of the suggestions which it recommended. Cal. State Papers, Dom., 1661–1662, p. 83.

[109] Cf. Cal. State Papers, Dom., 1661–1662, p. 83.

[110] Cal. State Papers, Dom., 1665–1666, p. 330. Yet Crispe's letter (*ante,* p. 75, note) certainly speaks as if the Council had a continuous existence from 1660 to 1668, and the mention of Exeter House as its place of meeting after 1667 points in the same direction.

ascribed "an infinite interruption to the whole trade of the Nation." The fire and the Dutch war completed the demoralization of commerce and in 1666 the plantations were deemed in great want of necessaries on account of the obstructions of trade by the war. Though in that year many questions arose that might naturally have been referred to such a council had it been in session, no such references appear among the records. The advancement of trade was looked after by the Privy Council and its trade committee, and particularly by the Committee of Trade appointed by Parliament. The latter body had been named as early as March, 1664, to investigate the export of wool, wool-fells, and fullers' earth. A few weeks later it was entrusted with the duty of inquiring into the reasons for the general decay of trade. As this function was conferred on the Parliamentary Committee at a time when the Select Council was still holding its sessions, it is reasonable to suppose that the work of the latter body had not proved satisfactory. There is some slight evidence to show that the meetings of the Council were at this time but little attended and that its members were not working in harmony.[111] The Parliamentary Committee, acting as a Council of Trade, ordered representatives from all the merchant companies to prepare an account of the causes of obstruction in their different branches, and when the latter, among other obstacles, named the Dutch as the chief enemies of English trade, resolved that the wrongs inflicted by the Dutch were the greatest obstructions to foreign trade, and recommended that the King should seek redress. Other causes were considered and debated.[112]

Commission for English-Scottish Trade, 1667–1668

An excellent idea of procedure can be obtained from studying the history of trade relations with Scotland during this decade. Immediately after the passage of the Navigation Act of 1660, the Scots petitioned that the Act might be dispensed with for Scotland, and special deputies were sent from the Scottish to the English Parliament to prevent, if possible, the extension of the Act to their country. The matter was referred to the Customs Commissioners and to the Privy Council, and the latter appointed a special committee to investigate it. Both of these bodies reported that the grant of such liberties to the Scots would frustrate the object of the Act, and gave elaborate reasons for this opinion.[113] As an act of retaliation the Scottish Parliament laid heavy impositions upon English goods, and English merchants in 1664 petitioned Parliament for relief. Parliament recommended the appointment of referees on both sides and in July, 1664, the Privy Council placed the matter in the hands of Southampton, Ashley, and Secretary Bennet. This committee laid the question before the Council of Trade, which suggested a compromise, whereby duties on both sides should be reduced to 5 per cent., the Scots should have the benefits of the Act of Navigation but no intercourse with foreign plantations, and should not buy any more foreign built ships. As a result of these and further negotiations Parliament passed an act in 1667,[114] "for settling freedom and intercourse of trade between England and Scotland," and under the terms of that

[111] "Some considerations about the commission for trade," P.R.O. Shaftesbury MSS., Div. X, 8(1).

[112] Cal. State Papers, Dom., 1663–1664, pp. 528, 531, 543, 572, 573, 588.

[113] Cal. State Papers, Dom., 1661–1662, pp. 75, 135–136, 149.

[114] 19 Charles II, c. 13.

act commissioners were appointed to meet with commissioners for Scotland in the Inner Star Chamber to negotiate a freedom of trade between the two countries. The commissioners duly met on January 13, 1668, and the papers recording their negotiations are full and explicit. The whole question of the relations between England and Scotland since the union, both political and economic, was investigated with great care; papers were searched for, records examined, memorials and petitions received, and various conditions of trade inquired into. The commissioners frequently disagreed and harmony was by no means always attained, resulting in delays in drafting the treaty and the eventual failure of the negotiations. In October the Scottish commissioners returned to Edinburgh, and the conditions remained as before.[115]

Reorganization of Committees of the Privy Council, 1668

The fall of Clarendon, at the end of the year 1667, led to important changes in the organization of the government, and the widespread demoralization in trade demanded an improvement of the system of trade and plantation control. The year 1668 is significant as the starting point for a number of attempted remedies in matters of finance and trade supervision. We have no opportunity here to examine the political aspects of these changes or to determine how far they were effected in the interest of mere political control. Suffice it to say that too many conditions of the reign of Charles II have been attributed to extravagance and political intrigue, and too few to an honest desire on the part of those concerned to restore the realm to a condition of solvency and prosperity. Heavily burdened with debt at the outset of the reign, distracted by plague, fire, and foreign war during the years from 1665 to 1668, the kingdom needed the services of all its statesmen, and even the most selfish politician must have realized the need of reorganization. Acting upon a suggestion which Clarendon himself had made to the King, the Privy Council in 1667 began by strengthening its own committee system, and on January 31, 1668, established four standing committees—for foreign affairs, military affairs, trade and plantations, and petitions and grievances. These committees had almost the character of state departments, though they had no final authority of their own, all orders emanating from the Privy Council only. They became, however, more independent than had been previous committees by virtue of the fact that no order was to be issued by the Council until it had been "first perused by the Reporter of each Committee respectively," The following is a copy of the regulations:

> His Matie among other the important parts of his Affairs having taken into his princely consideration the way & method of managing matters at the Council Board, And reflecting that his Councills would have more reputation if they were put into a more settled & established course, Hath thought it fit to appoint certaine Standing Comitties of the Council for several Businesses together with regular days & places for their assembling in such sort as followeth:
>
> 1. The Committee of FORRAINE AFFAIRES is already settled to

[115] Cal. State Papers, Dom., 1667–1668, pp. 156, 158, 165, 173, 180, 187, 191, 247, 321, 433, 444, 452, 511, 593, 594; 1668–1669, pp. 35, 40.

consist of these Persons following (besides his Royall Highness, who is understood to be of all comittees, where he pleases to be) vizt. Prince Rupert, Ld Keeper [Sir Orlando Bridgeman], Lord Privy Scale [Lord Robartes], Duke of Buckingham, Lord General [Duke of Albemarle], Ld Arlington, & Mr Sec^{ry} Morice, To which Committee His Matie doth also hereby referr the corresponding wth Justices of peace & other officers & ministers in the Severall Countys of the Kingdome, concerning the Temper of the Kingdome &c. The constant day for this Committee to meete to be every Monday besides such other dayes wherein any extraordinary Action shall oblige them to assemble, And the place for their meeting to be at the Lord Arlington's Lodgings in Whitehall.

2. Such matters as concerne the Admiralty & Navy as also all Military matters, Fortifications &c, so far as they are fit to be brought to the Councill Board, without intermedling in what concernes the proper officers (unlesse it shall by them be desired). If his Matie is pleased to appoint that they be und^r the consideracon of this following Committee, vizt, Prince Rupert, Ld General [Duke of Albemarle], E. of Anglesy, Ea. of Carlisle, Ea. of Craven, Lord Arlington, Lord Berkeley, Mr Comptroller [Sir Thomas Clifford], Mr Sec^{ry} Morice, Sr Wm Coventry & Sr John Duncombe. The usuall day of meeting to be Wensdays, & oftner, as he that presides shall direct, & the place to be the Councill Chamber, and hereof Three or more of them to be a Quorum.

3. Another Committee his Matie is pleased to constitute for the Business of Trade under whose consideration is to come whatsoever concernes his Ma^{ts}: FORRAINE PLANTATIONS, as also what relates to his Kingdomes of Ireland or Scotland, the Isles of Jersey & Guernsey, which is to consist of the Lord Privy Scale [Lord Robartes], Duke of Buckingham, Earle of Ossory, Ea. of Bridgewater, Ea: of Lauderdail, L^d: Arlington, L^d: Holles, L^d: Ashley, M^r. Comptroller [Sir Thomas Clifford], Mr Vice Chamberlain [Sir George Carteret], Mr Sec^{ry}. Morice, & Sr Wm Coventry. The usuall day of meeting to be every Thursday in the Councill Chamber, or oftner as he that presides shall direct, and hereof 3 or more of them to be a Quorum.

4. His Matie is pleased to appoint one other Committee to whom all PETITIONS of COMPLAINT & GREIVANCE are to be referred in which His Matie hath thought fit hereby particularly to prescribe not to meddle wth Property or what relates to Meum & Tuum. And to this Committee his Matie is pleased that all matters which concerne Acts of State or of the Councill be referred. The persons to be the Arch. B^p: of Canterbury, Lord Keeper [Sir Orlando Bridgeman], L^d: Privy Seale [Lord Robartes], L^d: Great Chamberlain [?], Ld Chamberlain [Edward, Earl of Manchester], Ea: of

Bridgewater, Ea: of Anglesey, Ea: of Bathe, Ea: of Carbery, Viscount Fitzharding, L^d: Arlington, L^d: Holles, L^d: Ashley, Mr Sec^ry: Morice, M^r: Chancellor of the Dutchy [of Lancaster, Sir Thomas Ingram], and S^r: John Duncombe. The constant day of meeting to be Friday in the Councill Chamber. And his Ma^ts further meaning is, that to these two last committees, any of the Councill may have Liberty to come & vote and that his two principall Sec^ries: of State [at this time Lord Arlington and Sir William Morrice] be ever understood to be of all Com^tees:, And hereof 3 or more of them to be a Quorum.

And for the better carrying on of Business at those severall Comittees, his Matie: thinks fit, and accordingly is pleased to appoint, That each of these Committees be assigned to the particular care of some one person, who is constantly to attend it. In that of the Navy & Military matters his Royal Highness may p^rside, if he so please, or else the Lord Generall [Duke of Albemarle]. In Forraine matters the Ld Arlington. In Trade & Plantations the L^d: Privy Seale [Lord Robartes]. In matters of State & Greivances, the Lord Keeper [Sir Orlando Bridgeman].

Besides which fixt & established Committees, if there shall happen anything extraordinary that requires Advice, whether in matters relating to the Treasury, or of any other mixt nature other than what is afore determined His Maties meaning and intention is, that particular Committees be in such Cases appointed for them, as hath been accustomed. And that such Committees do make their Report in Writing, to be offered to his Matie: the next Councill day following, in which, if any Debate arise, the old Rule is ever strictly to be observed, that the youngest Councel- l^r: do begin, and not to speake a second time without Leave first obteyned. And that as on the one side nothing is hereafter to be resolved in Councill, till the matter hath been first examined, And have received the Opinion of some Committee or other, So on the other hand, that nothing be referred to any Committee, untill it have been first read at the Board, except in Forraine Affaires. And his Ma^ts express pleasure is, That no Order of Councill be henceforth any time issued out by the Clerks of the Councill till the same have been first perused by the Reporter of each Committee respectively.[116]

---

[116] Brit. Mus., Egerton MSS., 2543, ff. 205–205^b. Endorsed "Regulation of Committees of the Councill. Read & Ordered in Councill the 31st January, 1667^b." For reasons that cannot be explained this regulation is not entered in the Privy Council Register. It is a similar order of February 12, 1668, P.C.R., Charles II, Vol. VII, pp. 176–177, but otherwise omitted. For this reason the document is here printed in full. Cf. Cal. State Papers, Dom., 1667–1668, p. 261.

Work of Privy Council Committee for Foreign Plantations, 1668–1670

New Select Council of Trade, 1668–1672

There is very little evidence to show that the Committee of the Council for Trade and Plantations played any very conspicuous part in regulating either trade or plantations during the years from 1668 to 1675, though a number of petitions were referred to it. Its most important report was that recommending the restoration of the province of Maine to the grandson of Sir Ferdinando Gorges, but even that matter was taken out of its hands by the further reference of the Gorges' petition to the Committee for Foreign Affairs. In 1668, it dealt with the restitution of Surinam to the Dutch and the settlement of Lord Willoughby's claims; with relief for Barbadoes after the disastrous fire which destroyed St. Michaels in April of that year; with the equipment of Sir Tobias Bridges' regiment in the same island; and with the liberty granted to certain Dutch ships of trading to New York despite the Navigation Act. In 1669, it considered a few petitions and reported on Gorges' memorial. After 1670 it did little, as far as actual evidence of its activity is concerned, but it is entirely clear that it had to transact a great deal more business than is recorded either in the Register or in the Colonial Papers.[117] Many of the questions that were referred to the Select Council of Trade and the Select Council of Trade and Plantations were first passed upon by this committee or were referred to it after the report from the separate body had come in. Furthermore, we know that in the case of this committee, as of similar committees of the Privy Council after 1696, many questions were never allowed to pass out of its hands, except as they were reported to the Council itself. Though not conspicuous, it was potentially active and quite ready in 1675 to take up the burden of colonial control that the King placed upon it.[118]

Even before it had begun the reorganization of its committee system, the Privy Council made known its decision to revive the system of separate and select councils which had probably been in abeyance since 1665. On September 23, 1667, it ordered its Committee for Trade and Foreign Plantations to take into consideration the advisability of revoking the commissions of the two councils of 1660,—which councils must, therefore, have been deemed still legally in existence—and of uniting these bodies so as to form a single select council for trade and plantations. To this end it instructed the secretaries of those councils, Philip Frowde and George Duke, to appear before it. For reasons that are nowhere found among the official papers this plan was given up and the decision reached to revoke only the commission of the Council of Trade and to issue a patent for a new body. Roger North, in his *Examen*, published in 1740, a work little to be depended on as far as historical accuracy is concerned, declares that this move was merely a piece of political manœuvering and never was designed to accomplish anything of importance for the trade or revenue of the kingdom. He says:

[117] For instance, there are among the Colonial Papers memoranda of proceedings at various sittings of this committee held between April 7, 1668, and February 18, 1669, relative to domestic, colonial, and foreign trade, that are not recorded elsewhere.

[118] Cal. State Papers, Col., 1661–1668, §§ 1685, 1712, 1759, 1769, 1791, 1870, 1883; 1660–1674, §§ 30, 66, 150, 184–186, 751, 837, 1226, I, II, III; 1320, 1353, 1390. Dom., 1668–1669, pp. 62, 201.

"The courtiers, for his Majesty's Ease, moved that there might be a commission to several of the greatest Traders in *London* to examine all matters of that kind, and to report their Opinion to the Council; upon which his Majesty might determine. This plausible project was put in Execution and the Leaders of the Fanatic party in the city [especially Alderman Love and Josiah Child] were the Commissioners; for so it was plotted. The great House in Queen Street was taken for the use of this Commission. Mr. Henry Slingsby, sometime Master of the Mint was the Secretary; and they had a formal Board with Green Cloth and Standishes, Clerks good store, a tall Porter and Staff, and fitting Attendance below, and a huge Luminary at the Door. And in Winter Time, when the Board met, as was two or three Times a Week, or oftener, all the Rooms were lighted, Coaches at the Door, and great passing in and out, as if a Council of State in good Earnest had been sitting. All Cases, Complaints, and Deliberations of Trade were referred to this Commission, and they reported their opinion."[119]

North's implication that the Council was a contrivance of the enemies of the King to effect a prohibition of trade with France which the government wished to keep open seems deserving of little credence. In the past, facts regarding this Council and its work have not been complete, and even a full list of its members has been wanting. Even now the commission and instructions, which, after considerable delay, were issued on October 20, 1668, have eluded discovery, and we can present little more than the terms of the docket as entered in the books of the Crown Office. The docket reads: "A Commission with instructions annexed establishing a Counsell of Trade, for Keeping a control and super-inspection of his Majesty's Trade and Commerce." From another source we learn that the Council was to take into consideration "the Conditions of your Maj^{tyes} Plantations abroad, in order to the improvement of Trade and increase of Navigation, and for the further encouragement of yor Maj^{tyes} Subjects in their Trade and Commerce both at home and abroad."[120] A second commission was issued on April 13, 1669, "directed to the same persons in the same form & with the same powers and instructions ... with a confirmation of all Acts done in pursuance of the said late commission in election of officers and otherwise."[121] The clerical secretary was Peter du Moulin, though Dr. Benjamin Worsley seems to have had some official position on the board. The members of the Council were as follows: Duke of York, Prince Rupert, Lord Keeper, Lord Privy Seal, Duke of Buckingham, Duke of Albemarle, Duke of Ormond, Earl of Bridgewater, Earl of Ossory, Earl of Anglesey, Earl of Carlisle, Earl of Craven, Earl of Lauderdale, Lord Arlington, Lord Berkeley of Stratton, Lord Holles, Lord Ashley, Sir Thomas Clifford, Sir George Carteret, Sir John Trevor, Sir William Morrice, Sir William Coventry, Sir Thomas Osborne, Sir

---

[119] Roger North, Examen, p. 461, quoted by Prof. Ashley in Surveys, Historic and Economic, pp. 274–275.

[120] New York Colonial Docts., III, p. 175.

[121] P.R.O. Chancery, Crown Office, Docket Books, 7, pp. 335, 344; Cal. State Papers, Dom., 1668–1669, pp. 6, 18, 224–225.

Thomas Littleton, Sir Henry Blount, Sir George Downing, Sir Andrew Riccard, Sir William Thompson, Silas Titus, William Garroway, Henry Slingsby, Thomas Grey, John Birch, William Love, Esq., Benjamin Worsley, Doctor of Physic; John Buckworth, Thomas Papillion, John Page, Josiah Child, Thomas Tyte, Benjamin Albyn, and John Shorter. In 1669 were added the Earl of Devonshire, Earl of Sandwich, Viscount Halifax, and George, Lord Berkeley, making forty-six members in all.[122] This is an extraordinary body of men to be engaged in pulling the wool over the eyes of the King, and though Professor Ashley is inclined to view North's account with approval, we doubt if it will stand the test of examination. Professor Ashley's further belief that from this Council emanated the document called "A Scheme of Trade," is capable of satisfactory disproof, since but few of the signers of that document were members of the Council and the date when it was issued, November 29, 1674, was after the Council as a separate body had been abolished.[123]

The Council lasted from 1668 to 1672 and during that time it did nothing, so far as we can discover, either for or against the trade with France. It considered the granting of patents, foreign trade with Piedmont and elsewhere, the export of wool, disputes among the merchant companies, dispensations from the operation of the Navigation Act, and a few matters relating to home industry, particularly as regards abuses in the baize trade. It took into consideration the order in Council of October 23, 1667, permitting the Dutch to send three or more ships yearly for seven years to trade from Holland to New York, and reported so strongly against it that the Privy Council revoked the order.[124] More important still, it took up the whole question of the operation of the navigation acts in the colonies, called upon the merchants and the farmers of the customs for information, and made a careful report to the Privy Council, which the latter, on January 20, 1669, embodied in the following order:

> "His Matie this day taking into consideration the great importance the Trade of his severall plantations is to his Matie & his Kingdome, and being informed that severall Governments of the s^d Plantations have been wanting to their duty in the following particulars, viz:
>
> 1. That Governors have not taken the oath enjoined by law,
>
> 2. That shipps have been permitted to trade to and from the Plantations not qualified according to law,
>
> 3. That there has been omission in taking Bond and Security and returning those Bonds according as directed by the severall Acts of Parliament.
>
> For redresse it is ordered, that the Farmers of the Customs do and are hereby required (at their owne charge) to send over and

---

[122] Bodleian, Rawlinson MSS. A, 478, f. 77; Cal. State Papers, Dom., 1668–1669, pp. 224–225, 651.

[123] Ashley, Surveys, pp. 275–276.

[124] New York Colonial Docts., III, pp. 175–178; Cal. State Papers, Col., 1661–1668, §§ 1874, 1875.

make choice of upon the place & from time to time commissionate & maynteyne one or more persons in each Plantation (whom his Matie shall approve & authorize) to administer the usual oaths to the severall Governors, that no vessels be admitted to trade there till said officer has the perusal of the passes and certificates and certifies that they may trade there, and that no Bond or security be admitted without the allowance of said officer,

That letters be written to all said Governors to take said oaths before said officer and also to give them countenance and assistance,

That Directions be given to the Commanders of his Maties ships and to any merchant shipps to arrest any ship trading to His Maties Plantations contrary to the law."[125]

Under this order Edward Digges, former governor of Virginia and a London merchant well known to us, was appointed by the farmers of the customs as a fit person to execute for the colony of Virginia the articles and instructions contained in this order. No other appointments, however, appear to have been made at this time.[126]

After 1670 activities of the Council of Trade, as far as they are recorded, are very few. It considered the trade of the Eastland Company, provided for a supply of coal for London at reasonable rates, and discussed a few minor petitions, but as compared with its contemporary, the Council for Foreign Plantations, it accomplished little.[127]

---

[125] P.C.R., Charles II, Vol. VIII, p. 169; Cal. State Papers, Col., 1661–1668, § 1884, 1669–1674, §§ 6, 9.

[126] Cal. State Papers, Col., 1669–1674, §§ 104, 696.

[127] Cal. State Papers, Dom., 1671, p. 210; 1671–1672, pp. 450–451.

CHAPTER V.

THE PLANTATION COUNCILS OF 1670 AND 1672.

Influence of Ashley and Locke

During the years 1668 and 1669 no member of the government was more active in promoting the development of the plantations than Anthony Ashley Cooper, Lord Ashley. As one of the proprietaries of Carolina, he had taken the lead in advancing that settlement, had called upon John Locke to frame a new constitution, and had himself organized the expedition of 1669 which gave to the new colony its most important impetus. He became a proprietary of the Bahamas in 1670 and later attempted to found a plantation on the Edisto River. He planned to organize these colonies at Charles Town, Albemarle, Edisto, and New Providence into a kind of cooperative trading group of settlements, under the same laws and instructions, and from them he hoped to obtain in time for himself and the other proprietaries ample returns on their investments. It is of no concern to us here that his scheme failed, the important fact remains that Ashley and Locke were at this juncture in the very heyday of their interest in colonial affairs and were eager to take advantage of every opportunity for encouraging colonial trade. The revival of the Select Council for Foreign Plantations was due in largest part to the influence and initiative of these two men, particularly of Ashley, who in 1670 was at the height of his political power and on terms of closest intimacy with the King.[128] That he was sincere in this movement seems to me beyond question, and the charge that has been made against him of recommending the creation of this Council as a means of obtaining sinecures for his friends, does not appear capable of the slightest proof.[129] If membership on the Council was deemed at the first a position of ease, it must soon have lost that character, for few committee men ever worked harder than those who looked after plantation affairs in the years from 1670 to 1674. This fact will appear as we examine the nature and extent of their activities.

Revival of Council for Foreign Plantations, 1670–1672

Membership

Experience with previous councils had shown that too numerous and fluc-

[128] See various papers among the Shaftesbury MSS., Division X, particularly 8, No. 4, "Ld Shaftesbury's Advice to his Majesty about Trade, etc."

[129] Edward Long, governor and historian of Jamaica, viewed the appointment of the Council as a piece of jobbery and graft, an undertaking espoused not for the national good, but in order to obtain new and lucrative offices for Ashley and others "his Brethren in the ministry." Brit. Mus. Add. MSS., 12438, iii, f. 17.

tuating a membership was not conducive either to harmony or to despatch of business. Therefore, in reviving the Council for Plantations it was decided, as the most important change to be effected, that the number should be reduced to such terms as to enable the committee to apply itself as a whole to the business in hand. The commission was issued on July 30, 1670, to ten persons, of whom but three were members of the nobility. The commissioners were Edward, Earl of Sandwich; Richard, Lord Gorges, Baron of Dundalk in Ireland; William, Lord Allington, Baron of Killar in Ireland; Thomas Grey, son of Lord Grey, of Warke; Henry Brouncker, Sir Humphrey Winch, Sir John Finch, Edmund Waller, Henry Slingsby, master and worker of the mint and one of the gentlemen of the privy chamber, and Silas Titus, one of the grooms of the bed chamber. To this number was added in 1671 James, Duke of York; Prince Rupert, George, Duke of Buckingham, Master of the Horse; James, Duke of Ormond, Lord Steward of the Royal Household; John, Earl of Lauderdale, Secretary of State for Scotland; Thomas, Lord Culpeper; Sir George Carteret, Vice-Chamberlain; and John Evelyn, but of these only the last named stood on the same footing with those first appointed as a regular and salaried member, the others being appointed to give weight and dignity to the board and receiving no compensation. In August, 1671, Sir Richard Temple was added to the board, also to serve without pay. The only basis for the charge of self-seeking which has been brought against the members of this Council is the fact that for the first time, as far as we know, the working members received pay for their services. The allowances and salaries were as follows: the Earl of Sandwich, as president, received £700; Lord Gorges, Lord Allington, Thomas Grey, Henry Brouncker, Sir Humphrey Winch, Sir John Finch, Edmund Waller, Henry Slingsby, Silas Titus, and John Evelyn, each £500, paid quarterly. Dr. Benjamin Worsley, who held the position of advisor and assistant secretary under Slingsby, the secretary of the Council, was allowed £300, while for contingent expenses £1,000, the same amount that had been placed at the disposal of each of the secretaries, Sir Philip Frowde and Col. Duke, of the former councils, was appropriated.[130] Five members, always including the president or one of the officers of state authorized to attend, constituted a quorum of the Council, which was ordered to meet for the first time at Essex House, the residence of the Lord Keeper, Sir Orlando Bridgeman, near Temple Bar, at two in the afternoon. After the addition of the new members, May 16, 1671, it removed to the Earl of Bristol's house in Queen Street near Lincoln's Inn Fields;[131] and after February 12, 1672, to Lord Arlington's lodgings in Whitehall,

---

[130] Henry Slingsby is named secretary and treasurer in the commission and his signature or initials are appended to all orders from October 5, 1670, to July 23, 1672. During this time and until September 13, 1673, Dr. Worsley acted as assistant and is called "secretary" until November 15, 1672, when he was made treasurer also. On October 15, 1673, after the discharge of Worsley, John Locke, secretary, friend, and ally of the Earl of Shaftesbury, president of the new Council of 1672, was sworn in as secretary and as treasurer on December 16, 1673. He remained in service until the abolition of the Council. Evelyn speaks of Worsley as dead on October 15, but this statement cannot be true as Worsley was still alive in March, 1675.

[131] Evelyn in describing the room in which the Council sat mentions atlases, maps, charts, globes, etc., but Locke when called upon to hand over the papers in March, 1675, reported that he never had had any globes and maps.

in order, as Evelyn tells us, that the King might be present and hear the debates. It was authorized to employ clerks, messengers, solicitors, doorkeepers, and other inferior officers and attendants as it should think fit and necessary for its service.

Commission and Instructions

By their commission the members of the Council were empowered "to inform themselves by the best ways and meanes they can of the present State and condition of our Plantations, together with the Increase, or Decay of the Trade, and strength of each of them respectively, And the Causes and Reasons of such Encrease or Decay, And to use all Industry and Diligence for gaining the full knowledge of all things transacted within any part of those our Dominions, either by the respective Governours themselves or their respective Deputies or by them and the respective Councills, or Assemblies, belonging to any of our said respective Plantations, and thereof from time to time to give us a true faithfull and certaine Accompt togeather with their best advice and opinion thereupon." The range of colonial interest was a wide one, "all the affaires which doe or may touch or concerne any of our Forreigne Plantations, Colonies, or Dominions, situate, lying and being in any part of America or in the Ocean lying betweene this and the maine Land of America, or in any part of the Bay of Mexico, or upon the Coast of Guinea, or within any of that circuit of the Globe, that is generally known or called by the name of the West Indies, whether the said Plantations, Countries, and Territories, be immediately held by us, or held by any others of us, by vertue of any Charters, Graunts, or Letters Patents thereof already made or graunted, or hereafter to be made or graunted, and of all other and forreigne Plantations, Colonies, and Dominions (our Towne, Citty and Garrison of Tangier only excepted)." The Council had power to send for any person or persons whom it deemed able to furnish information or advice; to call for any books, papers, or records that it judged likely to be useful to it, and to require of every person called upon or colonial official addressed prompt and ready response.

By its instructions and additional instructions the Council was ordered to make full inquiry into the state of the plantations and to take every means of acquiring full and accurate information as to the powers of the governors, the execution of the same, the number of parishes, planters, servants, and slaves there, and the best means for increasing the supply where needed. It was to instruct the governors to live at peace with the Indians and not to suffer them to be injured in their persons, goods, or possessions; and to keep on terms of amity with their neighbors, whether Dutch, French, or Spanish; to take such measures that all commodities of the growth or making of the Plantations be duly manufactured and improved, and to inquire whether it were possible to promote in any way the production of such tropical commodities as cotton, ginger, cocoa, etc. It was to find out what islands were best fitted for the breeding of cattle and to encourage the same; to investigate the opportunities of obtaining masts and to stimulate the production of hemp, flax, pitch, and tar in New England, and the setting up of saw mills. It was instructed to study the question of procuring servants and slaves, to settle all difficulties between the Royal African Company and the colonies, and to do all in its power to check "spiriting" or the enticing of children and young persons from

England to the plantations. It was to deal with colonial trade, both oceanic and coastwise, to see that the acts of navigation were duly enforced; to inquire into the conduct of colonial governments, to examine colonial laws and to recommend for annulment such as were contrary to honor, justice, or the law of England. It was to become familiar with colonial geography, to procure maps and charts, and to have them available for examination. It was to aid the spread of the Gospel, the purification of morals, and the instruction of Indians and slaves. By the additional instructions, issued August 1, 1670, it was to consider the question of colonial defence, to recommend the production of saltpetre, to consider how spices, gums, drugs, dyeing stuffs, etc., might be procured for the plantations from the East Indies, and to study the systems employed in other countries for the improvement of trade and the plantations.[132]

Meetings and Work

It is noteworthy that the sessions of the Council were held in secret, no one being admitted except the members, and even those only after each had taken an oath not to betray the proceedings. "You shall swear," so runs this oath, "to be true and faithful to our Sovereign Lord the King, his heirs and successors; you shall according to the best of your skill, discretion, knowledge, and experience give unto his Maj^{tie} true and faithful councell, in all things that shall be demanded of you touching or concerning his Maties forreigne Plantations. You shall keepe secret and conceale his Maties said Councells, without disclosing the same to any person except he be of the same Councill, and if the matter touch any of the same Council you shall not disclose the same to him. You shall not promote or further any matter in the said Councill, for any reward, favour, affection, or displeasure, And in case you shall perceive anything to be done contrary to his Maties honour and service you shall to the utmost of your Power with stand and Lett the same."

The Council had its first meeting on August 3, 1670, when the commission and instructions were read; and from that time until September 20, 1672, a period of nearly twenty-three months, it held one hundred meetings of which we have record, and probably many more of which no record has been found.[133] It is rea-

[132] The commission, instructions, and additional instructions of the Council for Foreign Plantations are to be found among the Shaftesbury Papers in the Public Record Office, fair written in an entry book bound in vellum. Div. X, 10. Another copy of the instructions is contained in X, 8 (11).

[133] The sources for the history of the councils of 1670 and 1672 are: The Calendar of State Papers, Colonial, 1669–1674, which contains abstracts of the papers of the Councils now among the Colonial Papers. Had it been possible to examine each original document before writing this paper there is no doubt that the list of the meetings given in the Appendix would have been considerably extended. The calendaring is often far from clear and the indexing, as far as all the boards are concerned from 1622 to 1675, is a muddle of confusion. Among the Board of Trade Papers is an Index to the entry books of the councils, which shows that the following books, "called in the stile of the office, the 'rough books,'" were kept: "A Journal," "Orders of Council of Foreign Plantations," "Petitions, References, and Reports," "Addresses and Advices," "Letters and Answers," "Miscellanies," "Barbadoes," "Leeward Islands," "Jamaica," "Virginia," "Letters from the Council," "New England," "Fishery," "West India, Surinam," and "Letters to the Council." Most of these entry books have been found scattered among the Colonial Office volumes. Unfortunately the

sonable to infer that during the working months the Council met twice a week.

The Council began by taking over much of the business left unfinished by the Committee of the Privy Council, but it soon increased its activity. It early inaugurated a policy and system of control that was more comprehensive than any which had been put into practice by the previous boards. Efficient though some of the former councils and committees had been, no one of them had endeavored to cover so wide a range of colonial business or to inquire so minutely into the details of colonial government as did this Council of 1670. It not only took into consideration all petitions, memorials, statements of claim, and subjects in dispute, but it also set up an elaborate system of inquiry on its own part, following out the instructions which had been given to it to require of every colonial governor frequent information regarding the condition of his government. It drafted long series of queries which were despatched to all the colonies, and to which elaborate replies were received, notably from Berkeley, of Virginia, Wheeler, of St. Christopher, and Lynch, of Jamaica. It supplemented the information thus received by demanding letters from the governors, and received in response long and frequent epistles, dealing with colonial affairs in the most minute detail. Wheeler, Stapleton, Lynch, Willoughby, Colleton, and others furnished the Council with all sorts of descriptive and statistical matter, and were always ready to offer suggestion and advice. Merchants, planters, agents, and others familiar with colonial trade were also called upon for statements, either in person or in writing, and at many a meeting outsiders were called in to make reports to the board. The evidence thus obtained was generally discussed in the Council itself, at which the King and officers of state were occasionally present, and it was also referred to committees of two or more, which made their report to the Council. Upon the information and opinions thus obtained, the Council based its orders and reports to the Privy Council.[134]

In addition to these functions, the Council assumed an important and in some ways a new rôle when it took upon itself the business of preparing all the preliminary drafts of the various commissions and instructions of the governors, often spending many days in the consideration of these instruments, and often receiving from the appointees themselves suggestions as to the wording of certain clauses. As far as the more general powers and duties were concerned, these instructions were modelled somewhat after those which the Council itself had received, and lively debate arose not infrequently over the nature and extent of the authority that ought to be conferred on the appointees. The drafts of the commission and most important book, "A Journal," is missing and has been missing for two centuries. The "Index," however, contains a series of entries entitled, "Heads of Business," which is very incomplete as an index to the meetings, but upon which I have drawn in making up my list. The "Virginia" volume is also missing, but it apparently contained nothing except blank leaves. Part one of the volume entitled "Letters and Answers" and the whole of "Letters to the Council" are also missing. The "New England" volume contains only a copy of the Massachusetts charter; that entitled "Miscellaneous" three interesting papers "Concerning Spiriting," "Consideration about Foreign Plantations," and "Other considerations concerning Plantations." The complete minutes of two meetings are among the Shaftesbury Papers and very interesting notes in Evelyn's Diary.

[134] Cal. State Papers, Col., 1669–1674, §§ 327, I, 415, 565, 663, 680, 697, 704, 737, 804, 805, 891, 896, 1044, 1101.

instructions, when completed, were sent to the Secretary of State, by whom corrections might be made, then conveyed to the Privy Council, where the documents were frequently referred to the attorney general for his advice on legal points, and sometimes to the Committee of the Council, which at this time, as well as afterward, felt itself fully empowered to make any alterations it pleased. Thus many hands may have had a share in shaping these important papers before they were finally engrossed, although it is probable that in the majority of instances the draft of the Council was accepted unchanged by the King.

The Council was also beginning to exercise another important function in receiving from the Privy Council copies of laws passed in the colonies upon the character of which its opinion was desired, and in being called upon by the Privy Council or the Secretary of State to make recommendations as to fit persons to hold colonial offices. In this particular, the most responsible task of the Council lay in the selection and instruction of special commissioners, who in accordance with many earlier precedents were vested with authority to go to the colonies for the settlement of difficult questions there. Three such commissions were set on foot by the Council of Plantations: that appointed to bring to an end the dispute with the French at St. Christopher; that appointed to treat with the Dutch regarding the English subjects at Surinam; and that designed for New England, which was to be openly commissioned to settle boundary disputes, but to be secretly instructed to inform the Council of the condition of the New England colonies, "and whether they were of such power as to be able to resist his Majesty and declare for themselves as independent of the Crown." No commissioners were, however, sent until the time of Edward Randolph.[135]

A large amount of time was consumed by the Council in considering the petitions and memorials of private persons, who had some grounds of complaint against one or other of the colonial governments. Among these the charges of Mason and Gorges against Massachusetts hold prominent place, but other complainants were none the less insistent; Capt. Archibald Henderson, of Antigua, who had been imprisoned by Governor Wheeler for alleged seditious practices; the owners of the ship *James*, of Belfast, which had been seized by Wheeler as a "stranger-built" trading contrary to the Navigation Acts; the owners of the logwood ship *William and Nicholas*, also seized by Wheeler on suspicion that it had obtained its lading in violation of the treaty of 1670 with Spain; owners of the *Peter*, of London, seized by the Spaniards in violation of the same treaty; Jamaica planters who claimed that Spain had broken the clause of the treaty relating to logwood cutting at Campeachy; one Mark Gabry, exporter of wool; merchants in Jamaica complaining of the number of Jews there and their engrossment of trade; inhabitants of Easthampton, Southampton, and Southold in Long Island in regard to their whale fishery and their relations with the Dutch at New Amsterdam; the government of Virginia against the Arlington and Culpeper grant. The Council also discussed many other matters, all more or less closely bound up with the welfare of the plantations and of plantation trade, such as the despatch of their letters and orders; the proper time for the sailing of merchant ships in order that

[135] Cal. State Papers, Col., 1669–1674, §§ 287, 365, 822, 834, 917, 1003, 1011–1013, 1100, 1186, 1197, 1212, 1251–1252, 1255, 1295, 1300, 1306, 1386.

advantage might be taken of companies or convoys; the sugar question in the West Indies, notably Barbadoes, that perennial cause of dispute from the point of view of customs and impositions; the enticing or spiriting away of young people from England to go as servants to the plantations, a grievance almost as old as the plantations themselves and one which Ashley had made a special subject of inquiry with the result that Parliament passed an Act, March 18, 1670, making "spiriting" a capital offence; the fisheries and the abuses in the Newfoundland trade; privateering, especially in relation to the act of Governor Modyford in commissioning Capt. Morgan to cruise against the Spaniards and to capture Panama; the slave trade and the relations of the plantations with the Royal African Company; and lastly, in obedience to the fourth article of its additional instructions, the proper supplying of the West India colonies with such commodities as silk, galls, spices, senna and other dyeing materials, in order to see whether or not such things could be obtained from the plantations, a subject upon which Dr. Worsley, who had already experimented with senna, was deemed an authority.

Select Council of Trade and Foreign Plantations, 1672–1674

Membership

The efficiency of the Council of Foreign Plantations and the inefficiency of the Council of Trade during the same period may well have led to the belief that the work would be better done if the functions of the latter were transferred to the former body. The death of the Earl of Sandwich, who lost his life in the naval engagement of Southwold Bay with De Ruyter, May 28, 1672, may have hastened this conclusion, and the need of economy, especially manifest in this year, 1672, may have been a further influence. Whatever the causes, as early as the summer of 1672 the decision was reached, undoubtedly through the advice of Lord Ashley, now the Earl of Shaftesbury, to reconstitute the Council, and to issue a new patent which should cover trade as well as foreign plantations. Evelyn says that the old Council met at Shaftesbury's house on September 1, 1672, to consider the draft of the new commission. The form of the commission having been approved, the warrant was issued to the attorney general on September 16 to prepare the bill for the King's signature, and on the twenty-seventh the Council was duly commissioned by writ of privy seal. The membership remained the same as before, with the single exception that the Earl of Shaftesbury took the place of the Earl of Sandwich as the president of the board, with Lord Culpeper as vice-president. When in December of the same year Sir John Finch was appointed ambassador to the Ottoman Empire, in place of Sir Daniel Harvey, deceased, Sir William Hickman was constituted a member of the Council in his stead. As in the case of the former Council, the Duke of York, Prince Rupert, and the chief officers of state were authorized to attend and vote but without pay. To their number were now added the Duke of Ormond, George, Viscount Halifax; Sir Thomas Osborne, and Sir Robert Long, all of whom, except Long, had been members of the Council of Trade, while Halifax, who had just returned from an important mission to France and was rapidly rising to power, had been a member of the committee of the House of Lords, appointed in October, 1669, to consider the improvement of trade. Sandwich and Shaftesbury had both been on the same committee, and it is not unlikely that the latter was responsible for the remarkable report made by this committee to the Lords that "some relaxation in ecclesiastical matters will be a means of improving the trade of this kingdom."[136]

Commission and Instructions

According to its commission, the Council of Trade and Plantations was "to take care of the welfare of our said Colonies and Plantations and of the Trade and Navigation of these our Kingdomes and of our said colonies and plantations," and was to be a council of advice to the King "in and for all the affairs which do or may any way concern the navigation, commerce, or trade, as well domestic as foreign of these our kingdoms and our said foreign colonies and plantations." Five were to constitute a quorum of which the president or vice-president or one of the unsalaried members should always be one. The salary of the president was raised to £800, that of the vice-president was made £700, while that of the other salaried members remained as before, £500. No treasurer or secretary is named in the commission, but Dr. Worsley held these offices until in September, 1673, he was discharged and John Locke took his place. In all other respects the commission of 1672 reproduces that of 1670.

The most noteworthy difference between the two councils is to be found in the instructions, which for the Council of 1672 form a very comprehensive and intelligent statement of the essentials of plantation control. The draft was undoubtedly written by Shaftesbury and Locke, for a preliminary sketch is to be found among the Shaftesbury Papers; the preliminary meeting for the consideration and approval of the articles was held at Shaftesbury's residence, Exeter House; and the essential portions of the document are all to be found embodied in one form or another in the instructions and suggestions sent to the planters in the Bahamas and Carolina, colonies which for two years had been a kind of experimental station for Shaftesbury's and Locke's ideas. All the later commissions and instructions were based in the main on the principles laid down in these documents, and neither the Lords of Trade from 1675 to 1696 nor the Board of Trade from 1696 to 1782 ever in any important particular passed the limits herein defined. Probably the instructions of 1672 became from this time forward the precedent and guide for those who in later years were called upon to shape the powers vested in the boards of trade and plantations. It frequently happened, of course, that orders in Council directed the attention of the boards to matters which needed special examination, but in the main it may be said that Povey first and Shaftesbury afterward mapped out the lines to be followed by future commissions in their control of plantation affairs. This fact gives to the work of these men a peculiar interest and value.

By the terms of the instructions of 1672, the Council was to consider first of all the trade of the kingdom and of the plantations in the following particulars: the increase and improvement of raw commodities for use at home, the promotion of manufactures, the betterment of the fishing trade at home and abroad, the opening of rivers, ports, and harbors, the proper distribution of trade and manufactures, the obstacles that lay in the way of English trade as compared with those confronting the trade of other nations, and all abuses of trade and manufactures

[136] Lord's Journal, XII, pp. 254, 257, 273–274, 284.

in the kingdom. It was to inquire into the best methods of increasing the sale and export of native commodities and manufactures, of encouraging the importation of foreign goods at the cheapest rates, of building ships for the carrying of such bulky articles as masts and timber, of extending correspondence with the great commercial centers abroad, and of opening free ports where foreign commodities might be landed and stored with small charge if designed for reëxportation. It was also to take into special consideration the advantages of a more open and free trade than that of companies and corporations, and to encourage inventions and improvements designed to improve any art, trade, or manufacture or to secure and promote trade and navigation.

Meetings and Work

So far as the plantations were concerned, the Council was to inquire into the general state of the colonies, and to obtain full information regarding councils, assemblies, courts of judicature, courts of admiralty, legislative and executive powers, statutes, laws and ordinances, militia, fortifications, arms, and ammunition. It was to learn all it could about boundaries, lands, mines, staple products, and manufactures; to determine whether or not nutmegs, cinnamon, cloves, pepper, and other spices would grow if planted; to inform itself regarding rivers, harbors, and fishing banks; and to estimate how many planters and parishes there were, how many whites and blacks yearly arrived, and how many people died each year. It was to learn the number of ships trading to the plantations, to discover the obstacles to trade and how they could be removed, the advantages and how they could be increased; it was to concern itself with export and import dues, public revenues, measures taken for the instruction of the people and the maintenance of the ministry. It was especially instructed to keep in frequent correspondence with the governors, to urge upon them the necessity of maintaining peace with their neighbors, the Indians and others, of taking the Indians under their protection and of guarding their persons, goods, and possessions according to law. Furthermore, it was to procure copies of all necessary documents, to purchase maps, plats, and charts when needed, to study those portions of treaties made with other countries that related to peace and commerce, and to determine how far those articles had been upheld and performed. And lastly, it was to consider the practice of other countries in matters of trade, commerce, and the colonies, and to see how far such practices might be of value to England.

The Council had its first meeting on October 13, at Essex House, and there the commission was read and the oaths were taken. Soon after, it took up its abode at Villier's House in King's Street near Whitehall, which it rented of the Duchess of Cleveland for £200 a year. There it had a council chamber, an office for the clerks, two messengers, a porter, a maid, and a chamber keeper, all of whom were paid out of the £1,000 allowed for contingent expenses. We have record of seventy-six meetings held between October 13, 1672, and December 22, 1674, a period of twenty-six months; but it is quite certain that more meetings than this were held, inasmuch as the session-days were every Wednesday and Friday at ten in the morning.[137] So far as the plantations were concerned the Council did

[137] Cal. State Papers, Dom., 1672–1673, pp. 213–214.

little more than continue the work of its predecessor, the Council of 1670, but in addition it concerned itself with a large number of questions that had to do with domestic and foreign as well as with colonial trade. The most important of these related to the petition of the English consul at Venice that his consulage be levied on goods and not on ships, a matter that aroused prolonged debate; to the petition of the Gambia adventurers against the importation by the East India Company of the dyeing wood called "sanders" which, because cheaper, was taking the place of their redwood from Africa; to the ordinances issued in Sweden against the English "privileges" concerning naval stores; to the exportation of wool from England, a matter already dealt with in an Act of Parliament; and to the treatment of merchants at the hands of the Spaniards, regarding which a number of petitions had been received by the board. A few new petitions were taken into consideration from traders and others in the plantations, notably those of the Jew Rabba Couty, whose ship had been seized at Jamaica on the ground that he was a foreigner; of William Helyar, whose woodland in Jamaica had been seized by Governor Lynch; of John Rodney and his wife Frances, whose plantation in Nevis had been seized by Governor Russell, a case destined to drag on for nearly two years.

In recommending the appointment of governors and other officials, passing upon colonial laws, scrutinizing nominations as of colonial councillors, corresponding with the governors, organizing an efficient system of communication and supervision in all matters touching trade and commerce, and in making reports to the King in Council,—in short, in the control and management of colonial affairs, the Council of 1672 placed the British colonial policy on a broader and more comprehensive foundation than had hitherto been laid and inaugurated a more thorough system of colonial control than had been established by any of its predecessors. It is doubtful if even the Lords of Trade or the Board of Trade surpassed the Councils of 1670 and 1672 in enthusiasm, loyalty, or dispatch of business.

Causes of the Revocation of the Commission of Select Council, 1674

On December 21, 1674, Charles II revoked the commission of the Council, and plantation affairs under their cognizance thus being "left loose and at large" were "restored to their accustomed channel of a Committee of the Privy Council," that is, to the Committee of the Board appointed for matters relating to Trade and Foreign Plantations.[138] The reasons for this step are of course to be found in the first instance in the fall of Shaftesbury from power the summer before, but that event is not in itself a sufficient explanation of the change. At least it is worthy of remark that the dissolution of the Council took place many months after Shaftesbury's dismissal. Probably a further cause is to be found in the widespread demand for economy and retrenchment. The Council of 1672 cost the King nearly £8,000 a year; the Committee of the Privy Council cost the King nothing for the services of its members, although its contingent expenses ran higher than had those of any previous board, amounting to between £275 and £400 a quarter from 1676 to 1687

---

[138] New York Col. Docts., III, pp. 228, 229–230; Cal. State Papers, Col., 1675–1676, §§ 648, 649.

and £250 and £300 from 1689 to 1696.[139]

Later History of Plantation Control, 1675–1782

Probably a greater reason for the dissolution of the Council of 1672 is to be found in the dissatisfaction which existed with the system of advisory and independent bodies. Povey expressed the matter well when he wrote:

> "His Matie since his happy Restoraton, rightly considering of how great Consequence his foreign Plantations are to this Crowne, hath at several times Commissionated certain select persons to be Councells for the Plantations, every one of which Councels were variously framed, instructed and encouraged, wch have all expired without any considerable advantage, or satisfaction to his Matie or the Plantations. Among the other Reasons wch may be given, why they proved fruitless, it seems, That it is found by experience that whatsoever Council is not enabled as well to execute as advise, must needs produce very imperfect and weak effects. It being, by its subordination and impotency obliged to have a continual recourse to superior Ministers, and Councels filled with other business, wch ofttimes gives great and prejudicial delays and usually begets new or slower deliberations and results, than the matter in hand may stand in need of, by wch means the authority and virtue of this little Council became faint and ineffectual. Seeing therefore it hath been held at all times, that may distant Colonies, and the manifold Concernments thereof do require and deserve to be consider'd and provided for by some select persons as a Councel for those affairs, And that the wisdom of our Government admits not such a plenary Authority, but solely in the highest Council, it remains only as the best expedient, That Com^{rs} be appointed out of the Privy Council under the Great Seal, who may sit on some appointed day in every [blank] and sometimes an hour before the Councel shall sit, as occasion may call for it, to take consideration of any of the affairs of the Plantations, who may give direcions in ordinary cases, and in cases extraordinary may report to the King and Councel."[140]

We do not know when this paper was written nor do we know whether it ever came to the attention of the King and his advisers. Its recommendation was certainly carried out, when the King, taking into his own hands again the full control of trade and the plantations, issued a commission in February, 1675, placing the entire charge of these matters in the hands of the committee of the Council, which through all the changes of fifteen years had never ceased to exercise its functions of supervision and control of colonial affairs. This committee, known as the Lords of Trade, acted as a board of trade and plantations for twenty years and conducted its business with eminent success. Its membership was occasionally changed,

[139] Brit. Mus., Add. MSS., 9767, 9768, containing an itemized expense account of the Lords of Trade from 1676 to 1696.

[140] Brit. Mus., Egerton, 2395, f. 276.

though as a rule the work fell upon a comparatively small number of men who were in frequent attendance. After the fall of the Stuarts, King William continued the same policy, appointing a new Council Committee and resisting all attempts of Parliament to interfere.

Parliament, however, determined to obtain control of the management of colonial affairs, and as early as 1694 made an effort in that direction. Acting evidently under the influence of the merchants of London, who resented the fact that affairs of this character should be entrusted to "courtiers without experience," it took into consideration the appointment of a separate board, whose members should be chosen by itself. The first bill was thrown out by Parliament, but the matter was brought up at the next session in December, 1695. Strenuous efforts were made by a few of the leading out-ports, such as Bristol, to obtain, through their members in Parliament, a representation on the proposed board, in order to overcome "the growing greatness of London." During December and January the matter was debated with great heat in the House, and Bristol went so far as to send up a special delegation to lobby in its behalf. The proposal was defeated by the King's opposition to this attempt to encroach upon his prerogative, and a compromise was effected, in which the out-ports played no part. Influenced by the determination of the majority in Parliament, William issued a commission on May 15, 1696, to a separate Board of Trade and Plantations, the membership of which was, however, to be controlled by the Crown.

Of the history of the Board of Trade, thus established in 1696, little need be said here. The board passed through many vicissitudes in its life of nearly eighty-seven years. It enjoyed its greatest repute during the first fifteen years of its existence, falling into the hands of inferior officials and placemen during the era of Walpole and the first years of the supremacy of Newcastle. Granted new powers in 1752, it rose again to a position of prominence which it held for fourteen years, and it reached a climax in 1765, when it was made a ministerial executive office of government, as were the Secretary's office and the boards of the Admiralty and the Treasury, possessing full authority and complete jurisdiction in all matters relative to its own department. This position of independence was, however, soon lost. On August 8, 1766, an order in Council declared that all measures relative to commerce and the colonies should originate either with the King in Council, the Committee of the Council, or one of the principal Secretaries of State. This order, which evidently originated with Shelburne, Secretary of the Southern Department, that he might increase thereby his control over all colonial affairs, reduced the board to the position of an advisory and consulting body upon such matters as the Council might refer to it. Henceforth all estimates for colonial services and the direction and application of money granted thereupon, which had hitherto been transacted by the board, were resumed by the higher authorities. From this time the importance and influence of the board steadily declined until it was finally abolished in 1782. The control of the colonies during the period from 1768 to 1782 was assumed by the new Secretary of State for the colonies and remained in his charge until his office also was abolished in the same year.

APPENDIX

I.

INSTRUCTIONS, BOARD OF TRADE, 1650.

First.—They are to take notice of all the Native commodities of this Land, or what Time and Industry may hereafter make Native and advise how they may not only be fully Manufactured, but well and truly wrought, to the Honor and Profit of the Commonwealth.

Secondly.—They are to consider how the Trades and Manufactures of this Nation may most fitly and equally be distributed to every part; to the end that one part may not abound with Trade, and another remain poor and desolate for the want of the same.

Thirdly.—They are to consult how the Trade may most conveniently be driven from one part of this Land to another. To which purpose they are to consider how the Rivers may be made more Navigable and the Ports more capable of Shipping.

Fourthly.—They are to consider how the Commodities of this Land may be vented, to the best advantage thereof, into Foraign Countreys, and not undervalued by the evil management of Trade, And that they advise how Obstructions of Trade into Foraign parts may be removed; and desire by all means, how new ways and places may be found out, for the better venting of the Native commodities of this Land.

Fifthly.—They are to advise how Free Ports or Landing-places for Foreign Commodities imported (without paying of Custom if again exported) may be appointed in several parts of this Land, and in what manner the same is to be effected.

Sixthly.—They are to consider of some way, that a most exact account be kept of all commodities imported and exported through the Land, to the end that a perfect Balance of Trade may be taken, whereby the Commonwealth may not be impoverished, by receiving of Commodities yearly from Foraign parts of a greater value than what was carried out.

Seventhly.—They are duly to consider the value of the *English* Coyns, and the Par thereof, in relation to the intrinsic value which it bears in weight and fineness with the Coyns of other Nations. Also to consider of the state of the Exchange, and of the gain or loss that comes to the Commonwealth by the Exchange now used by the Merchants.

Eighthly.—They are (in order to the Regulating and Benefit of Trade) seriously to consider what Customs, Impositions, and Excise is fit to be laid upon all Goods and Commodities, either Native or Imported, and how the said Customs, Impositions, and Excise may be best ordered and Regulated, and so equally laid and evenly managed, as neither Trade may be thereby hindered, nor the State made incapable to defray the Publique Charges of the Commonwealth.

Ninthly. —They are to take into their consideration whether it be necessary to give way to a more open or free Trade than that of Companies and Societies, and in what manner it is fittest to be done; wherein, notwithstanding, they are to take care that Government and Order in Trade may be preserved and Confusion avoided.

Tenthly. — They are to inform themselves of the particular Ordinances, Orders, Grants, Patents, and Constitutions of the several Companies of Merchants and Handicraftsmen, to the end that if any of them tend to the hurt of the Publique, they may be laid down in such manner as the Parliament shall think fit.

Eleventhly. —They are to consider the great Trade of Fishing, and that not only upon the coasts of *England* and *Ireland* but likewise of *Iceland, Greenland, Newfoundland,* and *New England,* or elsewhere, and to take care that the Fishermen may be encouraged to go on in their Labors, to the increase of Shipping and Mariners.

Twelfthly. —They are to take into their consideration the English Plantations in America or elsewhere, and to advise how those Plantations may be best managed, and made most useful for this Commonwealth, and how the Commodities thereof may be so multiplied and improved, as (if it be possible) those Plantations alone may supply the *Commonwealth* of *England* with whatsoever it necessarily wants. (Inderwick, *The Interregnum,* p. 74 note.)

II.

INSTRUCTIONS FOR THE COUNCIL FOR FOREIGN PLANTATIONS, 1670–1672.

GIVEN AT OUR COURT AT WHITEHALL THE 30TH DAY OF JULY, 1670.

Preamble.

Forasmuch as our severall Colonies, and Plantations abroad, have by the Prudence of our Predecessors, and not without the great hazard, Charge and Expence of these Nations been respectively setled, and being so setled are become the proper Right and Soveraigne Posessions of us: And forasmuch as the said Colonies having upon severall Occasions readily exprest their loyalty and faithfulnesse towards us, have thereby the more engaged us, out of our Princely care, not only to take notice of them, but by all Wayes and meanes to endeavour the promoting of their Welfare and Increase, togeather with their flourishing Estate and condition, and more especially their Protection and Defence.

To inquire of the State of the Plantations, of the Powers and Instructions of the Governours how Executed.

1. You are therefore strictly to inquire and informe your selves, by the best wayes and meanes you can of the State and condition of all and every of our said respective Colonies, and Plantations, what it is, by whome they are respectively governed, and what Commissions, Powers and Instructions, have been graunted by us, or any way derived from us to that End, how the same have been duly executed and observed.

Miscarriages to be represented.

And if upon Enquiry or Examination you shall find any neglect, or miscarriage, to have been committed by any of the said Governours respectively, or by any of their respective Deputies, or that any such neglect or miscarriage shall hereafter appeare to you, that shall tend to the abuse of our Authority, or to the prejudice of our Interest, Or to the dammage and discouragement of any of our said Plantations, you are forthwith and at all times from time to time carefully to represent the same to us, that we may give such direction therein as the affaire shall require and as to our Princely wisdome shall be thought fitt.

To send for Coppies of Commissions and Instructions, and consider of them.

To give Directions accordingly.

2. And to this End you are to demaund of the said Governours respectively, or of their respective Deputies, the Coppies of all such Commissions and Instructions, as have mediatly, or immediatly been derived from us, or to procure and require the same from the Officers of Record, within this our Kingdome. Which having you shall cause them to be fairly transcribed and entred in a Booke provided for that purpose. That you may at all times be the better enabled to judge of the Duties of the said Governours respectively, and may Administer such directions to them, as may be suitable thereunto, and most agreeable to our service.

What Number of Parishes, Planters, Servants and Slaves are in the Severall Plantations.

3. And that you may the better provide for the Defence, Welfare, and Security of the said Plantations, you are diligently to informe your selves how all and every of the said Colonies and Plantations are inhabited (viz) What number of Parishes there are in each respective Goverment, and what number of Planters there be in each Parish and what number of Servants doe belong to the said Planters respectively, and whether the said Servants are Christians, or Slaves that are brought from other parts.

If thinly stockt to consider how they may be supplyed from other Plantations or from these Dominions.

And if you shall find any of the said Plantations to be so thinly and weakly inhabited as that it may endanger the losse of them, you are to consider how and which way they may most conveniently be supplyed either from some other of our Plantations, where they are overstored, or from any part of these our Dominions.

Not to give just Provocations to their Neighbours, Indians, or others.

To preserve Amity with them.

4. And forasmuch as most of our said Colonies doe border upon the Indians of severall Countries, or doe lye neare the Plantations of our Neighbours the French, Spanish, or Dutch, and that peace is not to be expected either with the said Indians, or with such as are our Neighbours, without the due observance and præservation of Justice to each of them respecively. You are therefore strictly in our Name to charge and Command all and every the Governours of our said Colonies respectively, that they at no time give any just provocation to any of the said Indians, nor to any of our said Neighbours, that are at peace with us, or their Subjects, but that they doe by all just wayes and meanes endeavour to preserve the Amity that is respectively setled betweene them, and to begett also for the future a good and faire Correspondency with them.

Governours to receive all Indians under their Protections.

5. And inasmuch as some of the Natives of the said Indians may be of great use to give Intelligence to our Plantations, Or to discover the Trade of other Countries to them, or to be Guides to places more remote from them, or to informe our Governours of severall Advantages, and Commodities that may be within or neare to our severall Plantations, not otherwise capable to be known to them, And may be many other wayes serviceable, either to defend or to succour and assist our Plantations. It is therefore our pleasure, and we doe hereby require you, to

give strict order to our severall and respective Governours, that if any of the said Indian Nations shall at any time desire to put themselves under the protection of our Goverment, that they doe receive them, And that they doe by all Wayes and Meanes seeke firmly to oblige them, And that they doe direct or employ some persons purposely to learne the languages respectively of them.

And that they doe not only carefully protect and defend them from other Indians, and from any that are the Adversaries of them. But that they more especially take care that none of our owne Subjects, nor any of their respective Servants, doe at any time any way harme them.

Not to suffer them to be injured in their persons Goods or Possessions.

And that if any shall dare to offer any Violence to them in their respective persons, Goods or possessions, the said Governours doe severely punish the said Injuries agreeable to Justice and Right.

6. And for the better Improovement of the Trade and Commerce of the said Plantations, you are as much as in you lyeth to take care, and to give such Rules and Directions therein, as you shall in your Judgement thinke best.

That all Commodities of their Growth or making be duly manufactured and Improoved.

That all the Commodities which are made and produce in every of our said Plantations, may be duly cured, Manufactured, Improoved, and made as Merchantable to the utmost as they may, to the end that they may not only be of the greater perfection, but of the greater value, worth and repute abroad among other Countries.

Whether other Commodities, then what grow at present, may not be planted and thrive, as Cotton, Ginger, Cocoa &c.

7. To which End you are to inquire and informe your selves aright. Whether there may not be some better Species even of those very Commodities which we now plant, Than what we yet have, as of Cotton, Ginger, Cocoa &c. Or whether there may not be some better and more perfect skill used, in some other places, for the husbanding, managing, and perfecting the said Commodities, than what we use at present.

To gaine the knowledge and skill of such, & impart them to the People.

And if you find the same to be so, you are to use all Endeavour possible to procure the said Species, or to gaine the Knowledge of the said skill, and to impart the same to the people of our said Plantations.

What Islands are fittest and most conveniently seated for breeding of Cattle.

8. And forasmuch as the Increase of Horses, and Cattle for Draught or for Victuall, are of very great use for the settling of new, and for the furnishing of old Plantations, And that there are severall Islands which as we are informed, are not so fitt for the inhabiting, or for the planting of any Commodity in, as for the breeding the said Cattle, and which may yet be the more easily setled, by how much they require the lesse people.

You are therefore to informe your selves, what Islands are scituate most convenient for that purpose, and to conferre with such Seamen and Captaines of Shipps, as have viewed and coasted along the said places.

To give Encouragement towards the effecting of the same.

And to consider accordingly of such Conditions, and to publish such encouragements, as that the same may be most probable to be effected.

9. And in regard whatever conduceth to the Increase of Shipping, must equally conduce to the Safety and strength of these Nations.

Whether Masts and other Materialls for Shipping may not be furnished from the Plantations.

And that not only Masts, but all other Materialls, as well for the building, as fitting out of Shipps of great burthen may as we are informed be plentifully furnished from some of our Plantations, if care hereunto were more especially used.

To encourage the producing of Hempe, Flax, Pitch and Tarre in New England: and setting up of Sawing Mills.

You are therefore more particularly to advise about this matter, with the severall Governours, and Colonies of New England, and to propound to them or receive their Opinion, what methods and course might be most fitt for the producing of Flax, Hempe, Pitch and Tarre in those Countries in most plenty. As also where Mills might be most conveniently placed and encreased for the sawing of Timber, and Planke, and how best we may ease the charge and promote the building there of great Shipping.

How the Plantations may be supplyed with Servants and Slaves.

10. You are to take into your Consideration, how all and every our said Colonies, and Plantations, may be best supplyed both with servants and Slaves.

To consider the differences betwixt the Guiny Company, and the Plantations, and to find out expedients of agreement.

That none of his Maties Subjects of these kingdomes be forced or Enticed away to the Plantations by any unlawfull Practises, but that they may be duly accomodated.

And what just Objections the said Plantations have against the standing and Priviledges of the Guiny Company, Or what complaints the Guiny Company doth justly make against any of the said Colonies. And to find out such Expedients if possible, that neither of them may lye under any Discouragements, or that at least neither of them may be permitted to injure or oppresse the other. You are also as farre as you may, to provide that none of our Subjects in these Kingdomes, be either forced or enticed away into any of our said Plantations, by any indirect and unlawfull practises, But that all such persons neverthelesse, as are willing, and that shall desire to be transported thither, to seeke a better condition there than what they have at present at home, may by all meanes be encouraged.

And that some Course be duly considered by you also how far the future Vagrants, and all such persons as are Noxious, and infamous for their Lives here, may be Transported, as that the forreigne Plantations may be accomodated with them, and these Kingdomes disburthened.

Correspondency with the Governours the better to understand their Government, Plantations, Complaints, Trade and Shipping, and the Increase or Decrease thereof.

11. You are likewise to order and settle such a continuall correspondence with all and every our said Plentations, and with all and every the respective Governements of them. That you may be able as often as you are required thereunto to give us an Account, not only of the Governement of each Colony, and of the severall Commodities which they respectively plant, but of their severall Complaints and wants also, and how you find their Trade respectively to increase or decrease.

To which purpose you are to require an Account to be sent you continually from time to time of all the Shipps that shall Trade into any of the said Plantations. And of the substance of what lading they import thither togeather with an account also what Shipps are freighted from thence and with what sort of Goods, and what quantity there is of each of the said sorts, and whether Consigned. That so the true state and condition of each Colony in reference to the Trade and Increase and Decrease of it, may be thoroughly and rightly understood.

To regulate the trade of the Plantations, so that they may be serviceable to one another, as well as to these our kingdomes.

12. And being thus informed you are further to apply your selves by all prudentiall wayes and Meanes so to Order, Governe, and Regulate the Trade of our whole Plantations, that they may be most serviceable one unto another, and as the whole unto these our Kingdomes so these our kingdomes unto them.

To take care of the due execution of the Acts for encouragement of Shipping and Navigation.

13. You are therefore to inquire into, and strictly to take care of the due Execution of the severall Acts for the encouragement of Shipping, and Navigation and that as much as in you lyeth, none of those good Ends and purposes, so much tending to the strength and benefitt of this Nation may be frustrated for which the said Acts were primarily intended and designed.

To require Coppies of all Charters and Graunts concerning any forreigne Plantations.

14. And to the End that nothing may be wanting to the said Regulation and that Justice may be equally distributed throughout all our said Plantations, You are likewise to take an Inspection into, and require a Coppy of all Charters, and Graunts that have been passed by us or by any of our Præedecessors, to any particular persons, or to any Societies, and Corporations of Men with reference to any of the said Plantations.

And more particularly to informe your selves what Goverments are held by vertue of any of the said Charters at present, and by whome.

To examine how the Ends of them have been pursued or neglected.

In case of any differences to endeavour the composing of them amicably.

You are likewise to examine what Causes, Covenants and Conditions, with relation to our selfe and to the Crowne are inserted in any of the said Charters or Graunts, and how the same have been performed, and how the Ends of the said Graunts themselves have been respectively pursued. Or how much on the contrary, you find they have been neglected, and our selfe præjudiced, and to report the same to us. And in case there shall any differences arise concerning the bounds, and Limits of any of the said respective Charters, or concerning the Priviledges, Rights, or Properties, which may be challenged by any by vertue of the said Charters.

Otherwise to state and report them to his Matie.

You are to endeavour by the best and justest meanes you may, amicably to compose and determine the same. But if the difference arising about any of the said Charters, shall have so much difficulty, as that the same cannot be friendly and amicably ended as aforesaid. In that case you are after Examination of it to state it to us. That we may give such Resolution thereupon as may be agreeable to Justice.

To send for Coppies of the Lawes now in force that if upon examination any of them be found contrary to honour, Justice, or the Law of England, they may be nulled.

15. And as you are not to permitt any of our Loving Subjects to be oppressed by any of the Governours of our said Colonies contrary to the Lawes that are in force, within the said Colonies respectively, so you are as carefully to examine, send for and require a Coppy of all such Lawes, as have been at any time made, and doe stand yet unrepealed within any of our said Plantations. That if any of the said Lawes be found inconvenient or contrary to the Lawes of this Land, or to the honour and Justice of our Governement, all such Lawes may be immediately nulled.

To procure Mapps and Charts of the severall Plantations, and to Register and keep them.

16. You are also by all Wayes and meanes you may to procure exact Mapps, Platts or Charts of all and Every our said Plantations abroad, togeather with the Mapps and Descriptions of their respective Ports, Harbours, Forts, Bayes, Rivers with the Depth of their respective Channells comming in or going up, and the Soundings all along upon the said respective Coasts from place to place, and the same so had, you are carefully to Register and Keepe.

To take effectuall care for the Propagating the Gospell in the Plantations, and for the providing and maintaining of a pious and learned Ministry.

To reforme the Debaucheries of Planters and Servants.

You are above all especially required to take an effectual care for the Propagation of the Gospell, in all our said Colonies and Plantations respectively, by providing that there be good Encouragem^t setled for the Invitation and maintenance of pious and learned Ministers, and by sending strict Orders and Instructions for the regulating and reforming the Debaucheries of Planters and Servants, whose evill Example doth bring Scandall upon the Profession of Christianity, and doth deterre such as are not yet admitted thereunto, from effecting and esteeming the same.

To invite and Instruct the Indians and Slaves in the Christian Religion.

And you are to consider how much of the Indians, or such as are purchased from other parts for Slaves, may be best Instructed and invited to the Christian Religion and Faith, it being both for the Honour of our Crowne, and of the Protestant Religion it selfe. That all persons within any of our Territories though never so remote should be taught the Knowledge of God, and be accquainted with the Mysteries of Salvation.

To write Letters to the severall Governours to informe them of his Maties great care of the Plantations in erecting this Councill as also a generall Councill for trade.

18. You are therefore forthwith to write Letters and to send them to the severall Governours of our said respective Plantations, or to their respective Deputies in all parts, wherein you are to informe them of our great care and signall grace towards our said Colonies, and of our erecting not only a general Councill for Trade, that might take cognizance of such things as may be their concerne, But of our appointing this Councill in particular which is employed only for the better care and conduct of them.

To require of them an Account of the state of their present condition and of what they judge necessairie for their Securitie, Encouragem^t, and accomodation.

You are therefore to require them, by themselves, or by the Assistance of the respective Councills or Assemblies of the said Colonies to send you an exact account of the State of their Condition at present, and of such particulars within these your Instructions as you shall in the first place thinke most necessary for them to answer or informe you of.

And that they doe further propound to you what they judge to be most immediately necessary either for their security, or for the encouragement, and accomodation of them.

To observe such other Instructions as shall be sent under his Maties Signe Manuall, and if further Powers be found necessary, the Councill to adresse to his Matie therein.

19. Lastly you are to follow such other Instructions concerning the Præmises, as shall be sent to you from time to time by us under our Signe Manuall.

And in all cases wherein you shall judge that further Powers and Assistance shall be necessary for you, You are to addresse Your selves to us, for our further pleasure Resolution and Direction therein.

Given at our Court at Whitehall the 30th. day of July 1670, in the two and twentieth yeare of our Reigne.

By his Maties Command

ARLINGTON

ADDITIONAL INSTRUCTIONS FOR THE COUNCIL FOR FOREIGN PLANTATIONS, 1670–1672.

GIVEN AT OUR COURT AT WHITEHALL THE FIRST DAY OF AUGUST, 1670.

To inquire concerning the Strength Fortifications and Military discipline of the Plantations.

1. You are also particularly to inquire and informe your selves of the strength of all and every of our Colonies, how they are respectively fortifyed, what the said Fortifications are, and how conveniently situated; as also to inquire how the Inhabitants of the said Colonies are respectively trained or disciplined.

And in what Posture they are to make a resistance upon occasion, against any sudden attempt or Assault, if it should be offred them either by the Indians, or by the forces of any other Prince or State that are their Neighbours:

Concerning the Stores of their Ball, Powder, and other Ammunition and the securing and præserving of them.

And what Stores they have of Armes, Ball, Powder or any other Ammunition respectively, and what care is further necessary to be employed, for the better Securing and præserving each of them, and to give an account from time to time of the whole to us.

To recommend to the Governours, the breeding and producing of Salt Petre.

2. And forasmuch as we are informed, that there are among severall of our Plantations, Grounds very proper for the Breeding and producing of Salt Petre.

And those so rich also that if they were improoved to the utmost, great quantities of that Commodity might be easily had from those parts, without sending into the Indies for it:

You are therefore very specially to Recommend this affaire to the Governours of such Plantations, where you shall be informed the Grounds are fittest for this purpose. And not only to require their care for the Improovement of it; but to send your Advice to them, and to receive their respective answer and opinion, how and in what manner they judge the same, may be best, and most speedily put in Execution.

The Planting of such Commodities as are most for the benefit of the Plantacons and to redresse all præjudiciall Courses of Planting.

3. And forasmuch as the greatest benefitt that can arise to any of our said Colonies, must be when the Planters of any of the said Colonies shall be able to improove their Labour or Ground to the utmost Profitt respectively.

Wherefore if the Sayle of any of the said Plantations shall be equally fitt for the producing as well of severall other Commodities, as for the producing of that which the said Colonie is accustomed unto.

And that the said other Commodities are such also as are of more profitt to be planted by farre then that which is usuall, And that doe not only grow in the Countries adjacent to the said Plantations, but are found by Experience to thrive well even in the very said Plantations themselves.

In this Case you are to take care that a Custome be not nourished to the præjudice of Trade, and of the said Plantations, But that you take order for the Planting, Husbanding and Improoving of that Commodity that is most profitable and most for the benefitt of the said Plantation. And to this End that you by Letters conferre with the Governour, or with the Assembly of the said respective Plantation, that some redresse may be made and some stopp put to such a præjudiciall Course, or Custome of planting as is aforesaid.

To consider how Spices, Gummes, Drugs, Dying Stuffes &c. may best be obtained from the East Indies, and other places, for the storing and enriching Plantations, and how to Reward the Undertakers thereof.

4. And forasmuch as the scituation of severall of our said Plantations is such, as that it seemeth very probable to us, they might be stored with many more Druggs, Gummes, and Dying Stuffes than what they now have. Yea with severall Spices, and other Merchandises as well from the East Indies, Turkie, and other places, as from severall of the Spanish and Portugeeze Plantations. You are therefor required to consider and advise what Commodities, in any of the Countries aforementioned or in any other that shall be considered by you, may be (as you Judge) best and fittest to transplant into any of our said Colonies (respect being had to their said severall and respective Climates). And how the said Commodities may easiest, best, and with least Observation, be obtained from the said Countries:

What methods are meetest to be used, or what Rewards fittest to be given, to any that shall runne the hazards and Expence of it, to undertake them.

And which may therefore the same, may be most probably soe effected, as that the Commerce mey be encreased, and the said Plantations enriched through it.

What Councills are established in other Kingdomes, and what Powers and instructions are given them for the improving of their Trade and Plantations and to consider the Advantages and Disadvantages thereof.

5. You are to informe your selves as farre as you may what Councills are Established in any other Kingdome for the good Governement, and Improoving of their respective Plantations. What Directions or Instructions, also, are particularly given to the said respective Councills, and what Policy, Method or Conduct is used by them with relation to the Strength, Trade and Increase of the said respective Colonies, or with relation to the people themselves that are sent thither.

And if you shall discerne such Methods and Directions to be good, or to be well founded in Experience and Reason, You are to consider either how the same may be aplyed to the Advantage of our owne Plantations, or how any Inconveniences that may follow from them may be by you prudently avoided.

Given at our Court at Whitehall, the first day of August 1670, in the two and twentieth yeare of our Reigne.

By his Maties Command
ARLINGTON.

III.

DRAFT OF INSTRUCTIONS FOR THE COUNCIL OF TRADE AND FOREIGN PLANTATIONS, 1672–1674.

The Commission and Instructions Were Issued on September 27, 1672.

To consider the Improvem^t of the Commodityes of these Kingdomes.

1. You are to consider how all Goods and Commodityes of the Production or Growth of these Our Kingdomes may be best Improoved. What other usefull Commodityes or Materialls for Manufactures there are which the Nature of Our Sayle with good Husbandry will beare, or that tyme and Industry can make Native.

To consider the Setting up of Manufactures.

2. You are likewise to consider the setting up and Improoving of Manufactures within Our said Kingdomes, especially of shipping. And such others as are most for the Employment of Our people of best use, and greatest Proffit to our Kingdomes. The Establishing of Such Manufactures in Townes and places most convenient for them. And to provide that all such Manufactures (especially our Old and new Draperyas) be truely made and fully manufactured at home.

The improoving of the Fishing Trade at home & abroad.

3. You are to consider how the Fishing Trade both at home and abroad may be encouraged and improoved to the best advantage.

The opening of Rivers, Ports and Harbours.

4. How Our Rivers may be made Navigable and Our Ports and Harbours more capable of receiving Shipping.

The Distributing of Trade and Manufactures.

5. And how Trade and Manufactures may be more fitly and equally distributed through Our Kingdomes.

To examine the Burthens of Trade.

6. You are strictly to Examine what Burthens the Trade of Our sayd Kingdomes doth at present Groane under both at home and abroad, more then the Trade of Neighbouring Princes and States.

To enquire into abuses in Trade and Manufactures.

7. You are to make due Search and Inquiry into the abuses practised among Merchants, Vintners, Wyne-Coopers, Brewers, Dyers, Apothecaryes, Goldsmyths, Refyners, Wyre-Drawers, Penterers, Hatters, Clothiers and other Trades and Manufactures within these Our Kingdomes, as also concerning Weights and Measures.

To consider of the better venting of Native Commodity's.

8. You are to consider how Our Native Commodityes, and Manufactures may be vented in greater Quantetyes, and with more Hono^e and profitt to Our said Kingdomes.

How forreigne Commodityes may be brought in at cheaper Rates.

9. And how forreigne Goods, and Commodityes may be brought from the severall places of their Growth or making in fitt and reasonable tymes, and at the Cheapest rates.

About building of Ships for the carriage of Bulky Commodityes.

10. You are to consider about the Building of Pinkes, Flutes, and other great Ships for the more convenient Carryage of Masts, Tymber and other Bulky Commodityes. And about setting them out (according as the place to which they are bound may allow) with fewer men and Gunns then usuall.

How Correspondencyes may be kept in places of great commerce abroad.

11. You are to consider how Correspondencyes may be settled and kept in all places of Great Commerce abroad for the better knowing with what proffit or Losse Our Native Commodityes and Manufactures are vented. And What Lawes are from tyme to tyme made or Trades new Erected in forreigne parts to the advantage, or Disadvantage of Our Trade or Commerce.

How free Ports may be opened.

12. You are to consider how Free Ports may conveniently be opened about Our Coasts for the Landing, and Storeing of Forreigne Commodityes. Giving leave to retransport them paying only some small acknowledgements. And of the severall Advantages that may arise unto these Our Kingdomes by Giving way (according to the Example of other Nations) to a more open, and free Trade then that of Companyes and Corporations.

To receive Propositions concerning Trade and Navigation.

13. And you are to receive and Consider all Propositions or Overtures concerning new Inventions or Improvements in any Art, Trade or Manufacture, or concerning the regulating or Securing of Trade, and Improoving of Navigation that shall be offered unto you by any person whatsoever.

To enquire into the State of his Ma^ts forreigne Plantacons.

14. You are strictly to enquire, and informe yourselves by the best wayes and Meanes you can of the State and Condition of Our said Forreigne Collonyes and Plantations. By whome they are Governed and what Commissions, Powers and Instruccons have been granted by Us, or by any of Our Royall Predecessors to that End, and how the same have been Executed and observed.

To enquire What Councills Assemblies and Courts of Indicature there are in them.

15. You are likewise to enquire and informe yourselves. What Councills, Assemblyes and Courts of Indicature for Civill and Criminall Causes there are within the said Collonyes and Plantations, and of what Nature and Kind.

What Courts of Admiralty.

16. What Courts of Indicature they have relating to the Admiralty.

What their Legislative and Executive Powers are.

17. Where the Legislative and Executive Powers of their Governments are seated.

What Statutes and Lawes they have.

18. What Statutes, Lawes, and Ordinances they have made, and are now in force.

What number of Horse and Foot.

19. What number of Horse and Foot they have and whether Trayned Bands, Bands, or Standing Forces.

What Castles and Forts and how provided.

20. What Castles or Forts they have, how situated and what Stores and Provisions they are furnished with.

What strength their Neighbours have.

21. What strength their Bordering Neighbours have by Sea and Land.

What Correspondency they keep with them.

22. What Correspondency they keep with their Neighbours.

What Armes Ammunition &c. have been sent unto them.

23. What Armes, Ammunition, and Stores have been sent unto the said Collonyes and Plantations upon our Accompt, when received, how Employed, and what part of them is there remayning and where.

What Moneys have been paid for Armes &c. and Fortifications.

24. What Moneys have been paid or appointed to be paid by Us, or Leavyed within the said severall Collonys, and Plantacons for and towards the buying of Armes, or making and Mayntaining of any Fortifications, or Castles, And how the said Moneys have been expended.

The Boundaryes and Contents of their Lands.

25. What the Boundaryes, and Contents of their Lands are.

What Mynes, Commodityes and Manufactures they have.

26. What Mynes they have of Gold, Silver, Copper, Tynne, Ledd, or Iron. What Commodityes there are of their production, growth, or Manufacture. What Materialls for Shipping and whether Salt-petre is or may be produced in any of the said Collonyes or Plantations. And if so, At what Rates it may be delivered in England.

Whether Spices, Gumms, Drugs if Planted will not thrive.

27. Whether Nutmegs, Cinnamon, Cloves, Pepper, and other Spices, and Gumms, Druggs and Dying Stuffs which now grow in the East Indyes, and are brought from thence may not be planted and come to perfection in some of Our Collonyes, and Plantations in the West Indyes.

What Rivers, Harbours &c. they have.

28. What Rivers, Harbours, and Roads they have, and of What Depths, and Soundings.

What Banks or Shoales for Fishing.

29. What Banks, or Shoales they have upon, or neare their Coasts for Fishing.

What number of Planters and Parishes.

30. What number of Planters, Servants, and Slaves, and how many Parishes they have.

What number of Whites and Blacks doe yearly come.

31. What Number of English, Scotch, or Irish doe yearely come, and what Blacks, or Slaves, are brought unto them.

What number of People dye yearely.

32. What Number of People doe yearely dye within the said Collonyes and Plantations both Whites, and Blacks.

33. What Number of Shipps doe Yearely Trade to and from the said Collonyes and Plantations, and of what Burthen they are.

What number of Ships Trade yearely.

What obstructions they have and Advantages may be gained to their Trade.

34. What Obstructions there are, and What advantages may be gained to the Improovement of their Trade and Navigation.

What Dutyes are Charged upon Goods imported, or exported.

35. What Rates and Dutyes are charged and payable upon any Goods or Commodityes exported out of the said Collonyes and Plantations, whether of their owne Growth and Manufacture or otherwyse. As also upon Goods imported.

What Publick Revenues doe arise among them.

36. What Revenues doe or may arise unto Us within the said Collynes and Plantations, and of what nature they are. By whome Collected, and how answered and Accompted unto Us.

How they instruct the People in Religion, and pay their Ministry.

37. And what Course they take about Instructing of their People in the Christian Religion. And what Provision is made for the Maintenance of their Ministers.

To consider which of the said Collonyes are not fully Planted.

38. You are to informe yourselves which of our said Collonyes and Plantations

are not fully Planted or Inhabited, and to consider how such of them may most conveniently be supplyed from others that are overstored with people.

How the s^d Collonyes may be serviceable to one another and useful to these Kingdomes.

39. You are to consider how our said Collonyes, and Plantations may be serviceable unto one another in relation to their mutuall Sustenance and Defence, and how they may be Governed to be of use and advantage likewise to these Our Kingdomes.

To Correspond by Letters with forreigne Governours.

40. You are to take care in Keeping frequent Correspondency by Letters with the severall Governours of Our said Collonyes, and Plantations.

To Charge them to preserve peace with their Neighbo^rs and to protect ye Indians.

41. You are hereby required in Our Name strictly to charge all and every the Governours of Our said Collonyes and Plantations respectively. That they doe not Give any just Provocation unto any of their Neighbours Indians or others that are at Peace & Amity with Us. But that they doe by all just wayes and Meanes endeavours to preserve such Peace and Amity and keep a good and fayre Correspondencye with them.

And if any of the said Indians shall desire to putt themselves under the Protection of the Governours, or Governments of our said Collonyes or Plantations, That they doe receive them with respect and Kindnesse, and Give them due Protection, and Defence in their Persons, Goods, and Possessions according to Lawe. And in case any Persons shall contrary thereunto offer any Affronts or Injuryes unto them, That the said Governours doe severly punish such offenders according to Justice and Right.

To procure Coppyes of all Grants concerning the said Collonyes &c.

42. You are to endeavour the procuring Coppyes of all Letters Patents, Charters, or Grants of any of Our said Collonyes or Plantations, or of any Part of them, passed by Us or any of Our Predecessors under the Great Seale of England, to any Person, Socyety, or Corporation of Men Whatsoever. And to informe yourselves whether they have been duely putt in Execution according to the Severall Grants, Clauses and Conditions, conteyned in them respectively.

To procure Exact Mapps of the said Collonyes.

43. You are likewise to endeavour the procuring of Exact Mapps, Platts, or Charts of all Our said Collonyes and Plantations with the Descriptions of their respective Rivers, Forts, Harbours, Bayes, and Roads.

To consider of the improoving of their Trade and Commerce.

44. And when you shall have received due Information concerning the perticulars in the foregoing Instructions. You are to consider of the best wayes, and Meanes for the encourageing settling, and Improoving the Trade, and Commerce of Our sayd Collonyes, and Plantations. And accordingly to offer unto Us your Opinions, and Advice thereupon.

To Examine if the Articles of Peace and Commerce with forreigne Princes have been performed.

45. You are to consider the severall Articles of Peace and Commerce that have been heretofore made between Us or any of our Royal Predecessors, and all forreigne Princes, and States, and to Examine whether the Priviledges and Immunityes by them Granted or agreed for the Benefitt and advantage of Our Merchants, have from tyme to tyme been carefully upheld and performed, And in case you shall find any Manifest Breach of them, or any Injuryes done to Our Merchants, or any Obstructions to Our Trade thereby, You are to represent the same to Us for Our Consideration.

To enquire what Councills of Trade &c. are settled in forreigne Parts and w^t Commiss^{ns} Instructions and Allowances they have.

46. You are to informe yourselves the best that may be, What Councills, or Courts of Indicature are Established in any forreigne Kingdomes or States for the well Government of their Trade and Navigation, and for the Improovement Settlement, and Defence of their Collonyes and Plantations. As also What Commissions, Powers, Authorityes, Instructions, and allowances they have Given and Granted unto them for the better carrying on of those Services.

To observe such other Instructions &c as shall be sent und^r his Ma^{ts} Signe Manuall and to addresse to his Ma^{ty} for further Instructions &c. if need be.

47. And Lastly you are required and authorized to observe and putt in Execution all such other Powers, Authorityes and Instructions (relating unto Our said Collonyes or Plantations, or unto the Trade, Commerce or Navigation of them, or of these our Kingdomes) as shall from tyme to tyme be sent unto you by Us under Our Signe Manuall.

And where you shall judge it necessary to have any further Powers, Authorityes, or Instructions for the better Carrying on of Our Service therein. You are to Addresse yourselves unto Us for Our further Pleasure and Direction.

IV.

HEADS OF BUSINESS OF COUNCILS, 1670–1674.

Council for Foreign Plantations, 1670–1672.

August 3, 1670.

Commission and instructions for a Council for Foreign Plantations read. (From the Index mentioned on p. 101, note 6, here cited as Journal.)

August 9.

Letter to Trinity House. (Journal.)

August 12.

Oath of Secrecy to the Officers. (Journal.)

August 16.

Petition of St. Christopher read. (Journal; Cal. State Papers, Col. 1669–1674, § 232, here cited as Cal.)

August 19.

Commissioners for St. Christopher agreed on. (Journal; Cal., § 232.)

August 22.

Report on St. Christopher's case. (Cal., §§ 232, 850.)

September 22.

Petition for a chief governor of the Leeward Is. (Journal; Cal., § 268.)

September 24.

Beginning of consideration of Surinam question. (Journal; Cal., §§ 60, 291, 486, 524, and passim.)

September 26.

Col. Lynch to be a committee at St. Christopher and afterwards to goe to Jamaica as his Maj. Lieutenant. (Journal; Cal., § 287.)

September 27.

Leeward Is. petition again read. (Cal., § 269.)

September 29.

Drafting of queries to Gov. Berkeley of Virginia. (Cal., § 565.)

September 30.

Jamaica & the Isle of Providence. (Journal; Cal., § 276.)

October 5.

Surinam, Jamaica, St. Christopher; Conveyance of Letters to Foreign Plantations. (Journal; Cal., Dom., 1672–1673, p. 295.)

October 10.

Surinam agreement with the two ships, 20,00011 damage at St. Christopher. (Journal; Cal., §§ 274, 292, 295.)

October 18.

St. Christopher order of summons to planters of Barbadoes and petitioners from St. Christopher to appear. (Cal., § 297.) There must have been a meeting on "Friday next."

October 25.

Draft instructions for Commissioners for St. Christopher for bringing off from Surinam English subjects, their families, and estates. (Cal., § 304.)

October 27.

Leeward Is. their Governor apart, Answer of Lord Willoughby read. (Journal; Cal., §§ 309, 327.)

November 1.

Surinam, names of Commissioners. (Journal; Cal., §§ 319, 320, 324.)

November 5.

Commission and instructions to Major Bannister for fetching off the English from Surinam. (Cal., § 850.)

November 8.

Peace with Spain. (Journal; Cal., §§ 334, 334 I.)

November 12.

Barbadoes imposition on Sugar. (Journal; Cal., §§ 332, 519, 520, p. 229, passim.)

November 15.

Order regarding 16th article of the treaty with Spain. (Cal., § 334.)

November 17.

Report on petition of Leeward Is., favoring the petition, despite Lord Willoughby's objections. (Cal., §§ 339, 850.)

November 26.

Sir Chas. Wheeler appointed governor of the Leeward Is. (Journal; Cal., §§ 327, 392–397.)

December 16.

Commission and instructions to Sir Thomas Lynch, Lieut. Gov. of Jamaica. (Cal., § 850.)

1671.

January 14.

Newfoundland, petition regarding the fishery. (Journal; Cal., §§ 362, 368, 369, 385.)

January 21.

Governors of Plantations to take the Oaths [of Allegiance?]. (Journal.)

January 28.

Continuation of Newfoundland Question. (Journal.)

February 9.

Consideration of proposals of Sir Charles Wheeler. (Journal; Cal., §§ 410, 412, 415, 420.)

February 14.

Wheeler's proposals regarding defence of St. Christopher. (Journal; Cal., §§ 412, 850.)

February 18.

Spiriting, kidnapping of young persons for transport to the plantations. (Journal; Cal., 1661–1668, Preface, p. xxvii et seq.)

March 2.

Continuation of Newfoundland question. Report on the petition. (Cal., §§ 362, 850.)

March 8.

Estimate sent (and probably received on same day) by officers of ordnance regarding ammunition, etc. for Leeward Is. (Cal., § 445.)

March 10.

Report on Newfoundland petition, made on March 2, read. (Cal., Dom., 1671, under Mar. 10.)

April 27.

Petition of Ferdinando Gorges read. (Cal., § 512; See Cal., Dom., 1671, April 27, Slingsby to Williamson.)

May 22.

Robert Mason's first petition to the Council; divers relations concerning New England, with observations of the commissioners lately employed there, read. (Cal., § 512.)

May 26.

"The Earl of Bristol's house in Queen's Street (Lincoln's Inn Fields) was taken for the Commissioners of Trade and Plantations, and furnished with rich hangings of the King's. It consisted of seven rooms on a floor, with a long gallery, gardens, etc. This day we met the Duke of Buckingham, Earl of Lauderdale, Lord Culpeper, Sir George Carteret, Vice Chamberlain, and myself, had the oaths given us by the Earl of Sandwich, our President. It was to advise and counsel his Majesty, to the best of our abilities, for the well-governing of his Foreign Plantations, etc., the form very little differing from that given to the Privy Council. We then took our places at the Board in the Council Chamber, a very large room furnished with atlases, maps, charts, globes, etc. Then came the Lord Keeper, Sir Orlando Bridgeman, Earl of Arlington, Secretary of State, Lord Ashley, Mr. Treasurer, Sir John Trevor, the other Secretary, Sir John Duncomb, Lord Allington, Mr. Grey, son to the Lord Grey, Mr. Henry Broncher, Sir Humphrey Winch, Sir John Finch, Mr. Waller and Colonel Titus of the Bed chamber, with Mr. Slingsby, Secretary to the Council, and two clerks of the Council, who had all been sworn some days before. Being all set, our Patent was read, and then the additional Patent, in which was recited this new establishment; then, was delivered to each a copy of the Patent, and of instructions; after which we proceeded to business.

The first thing we did was to settle the form of a circular letter to the Governors of all his Majesty's Plantations and Territories in the West Indies and Islands thereof, to give them notice to whom they should apply themselves on all occasions, and to render us an account of their present state and government; but what we most insisted on was, to know the condition of New England, which appearing to be very independent as to their regard to Old England or his Majesty, rich and strong as they now were, there were great debates in what style to write to them; for the condition of that Colony was such that they were able to contest with all other Plantations about them, and there was fear of their breaking from all dependence on this nation; his Majesty, therefore commended this affair more expressly.

We, therefore, thought fit, in the first place, to acquaint ourselves as well as we could of the state of that place, by some whom we heard of that were newly come from thence; and to be informed of their present posture and condition; some of our Council were for sending them a menacing letter, which those who better understood the peevish and touchy humour of that Colony, were utterly against.

A letter was then read from Sir Thomas Modiford, Governor of Jamaica; and then the Council brake up." (Evelyn's Diary, II, pp. 63–64.)

June 6.

"I went to Council where was produced a most exact and ample information of the state of Jamaica and of the best expedients as to New England, on which there was a long debate; but at length it was concluded that if any it should be only a conciliating paper at first, or civil letter, till we had better information of the present face of things, since we understood they were a people almost on the very brink of renouncing any dependence on the Crown." (Evelyn's Diary, II, p. 65.)

June 16.

Colonel Cartwright's papers concerning the New England Colonies read. (Cal., § 512.)

June 19.

Patent of Massachusetts read. (Cal., § 572; The Journal says, "Cartwright's report"; but this seems to be wrong as both Evelyn and the Calendar place Cartwright's report on the 21st.)

June 20.

"To carry Colonel Middleton [Capt. Thomas Middleton of the former Council for Foreign Plantations] to Whitehall, to Lord Sandwich, our President, for some information which he was able to give of the Colony in New England." (Evelyn's Diary, II, p. 65.) Probably no regular meeting was held on this day.

June 21.

Commission and instructions of the New England Commissioners read; Col. Cartwright heard (Cal., §§ 512, 566). "To Council again, when one Colonel Cartwright a Nottinghamshire man (formerly in commission with Colonel Nicholls) gave us a considerable relation of that country; on which the Council concluded that in the first place a letter of amnesty should be despatched." (Evelyn's Diary, II, p. 65.)

June 26.

Further consideration of the New England case. (Cal., §§ 512.)

"To Council, where Lord Arlington acquainted us that it was his Majesty's proposal we should, every one of us, contribute £20 toward building a Council Chamber and conveniences somewhere in Whitehall, that his Majesty might come and sit amongst us, and hear our debates; the money we laid out to be reimbursed out of the contingent monies already set apart for us, viz. £1000 yearly. To this we unanimously consented." (Evelyn's Diary, II, p. 66.)

June 29.

Sir Thomas Modyford, Panama. (Journal; Cal., §§ 209, 433, 504, 505, 577, 578.)

"To Council, where were letters from Sir Thomas Modiford, of the expedition and exploit of Colonel Morgan, and others of Jamaica, on the Spanish Continent at Panama." (Evelyn's Diary, II, p. 66.)

July 4.

"To Council, where we agreed to and drew up a letter to be sent to New England, and made some proposal to Mr. Gorges, for his interest in a plantation there." (Evelyn's Diary, II, p. 66.)

July 12.

Report on Gorges petition, recommending the sending of commissioners to New England. (Cal., § 439, I.)

July 17.

New England, Massachusetts. (Journal.)

July 24.

Robert Mason's second petition to the Council read. (Cal., § 512.)

"To Council. Mr. Surveyor brought us a plot for the building of our Council Chamber, to be erected at the end of the Privy-garden, in Whitehall." (Evelyn's Diary, p. 66.)

August 3.

Agreement about Commissioners to New England. (Cal., § 512.)

Address regarding sending two ships to Surinam. (Cal., §§ 596, 850.)

"A full appearance at the Council. The matter in debate was whether we should send a deputy to New England, requiring them of the Massachusetts to restore such to their limits and respective possessions, as had petitioned the Council; this to be the open commission only; but in truth, with secret instructions to inform us of the condition of those Colonies, and whether they were of such power, as to be able to resist his Majesty and declare for themselves as independent of the Crown, which we were told and which of late years made them refractory. Colonel Middleton being called in, assured us they might be curbed by a few of his Majesty's first-rate frigates, to spoil

their trade with the islands; but, though my Lord President was not satis-
fied, the rest were, and we did resolve to advise his Majesty to send Commissioners with a formal Commission for adjusting boundaries, etc., with
some other instructions." (Evelyn's Diary, II, p. 66.)

August 12.

Report concerning New England, a representation of the present state
of New England and the sending over of Commissioners. (Cal., §§ 512, 598,
850.)

August 19.

"To Council. The letters of Sir Thomas Modiford were read, giving relation of the exploit at Panama, which was very brave." (Evelyn's Diary, II,
pp. 66–67.)

September 9.

Commissioners (names of) to be sent to New England. (Journal.)

September 15.

"In the afternoon at Council, where letters were read from Sir Charles
Wheeler, concerning his resigning his government at St. Christopher's." (Evelyn's Diary, II, p. 67.)

September 19.

Council informed that the king had agreed to the sending commissioners and desiring instructions to be prepared against spring. (Cal., § 512.)

November 13.

Further information to Council regarding commissioners; Council to
treat with Mason and Gorges regarding sale of their estates in New England,
but not without the king's leave. (Journal; Cal., § 512.)

St. Christopher and Leeward Is. (Journal.)

Negroes, Leeward Is. (Journal; Cal., § 700.)

November 14.

"To Council, where Sir Charles Wheeler, late Governor of the Leeward
Islands, having been complained of for many indiscreet managements, it
was resolved, on scanning many of the particulars, to advise his Majesty
to remove him; and consult what was to be done to prevent these inconveniences he had brought things to. This business stayed me in London almost
a week, being in Council or Committee every morning till the 25th." (Evelyn's Diary, II, p. 72.)

November 16.

Mr. Gorges, New England. (Journal.)

November 20.

St. Christopher; Publication by Sir Charles Wheeler and answer of the Council. (Journal; Cal., §§ 657, 658, 659.)

November 24.

Report to the king on the same subject. (Cal., §§ 659, 850.)

November 26 (7).

St. Christopher: proclamation disowning Sir Charles Wheeler read. (Journal; Cal., § 661.)

Mr. Brouncker's conference with the French ambassador read. (Journal.)

"We ordered that a proclamation should be presented to his Majesty to sign against what Sir Charles Wheeler had done in St. Christopher's since the war, on the articles of peace at Breda. He was shortly afterwards recalled." (Evelyn's Diary, p. 73.)

November 28.

The Answer of the Planters of the Leeward Is. read. (Journal.)

Account of Jamaica, probably taken from Gov. Lynch's answers to queries. (Journal; Cal., § 663, p. 277.)

Heads of king's proclamation regarding St. Christopher. (Journal.)

December 7.

Report of the Council on the proclamation and the framing of something fit to be offered to the French ambassador. (Cal., §§ 675, 677, 850.)

December 11.

New England Case, Mr. Mason's account of the commodities of New Hampshire. (Journal; Cal., § 687.)

December 14.

Mr. Mason, the answer of the Council. (Journal.)

December 18.

Instructions to Mr. Slingsby to speak to members of Privy Council regarding patents to Massachusetts. (Cal., § 652.)

December 19.

Mr. Slingsby's report about a new governor for the Leeward Is. (Journal.)

December 20.

Draft of commission for governor of Leeward Is.; revocation of Wheeler's commission; report to king concerning Col. Stapleton, the new governor. (Cal., §§ 699, 707, 738, 740, 744, 804, 805, 850.)

1672.

January 22.

Commissioners for New England. (Cal., § 512.)

February 6.

Report of Mr. Gorges, "Commissioner for the province of Maine" read. (Cal., § 753.)

February 12.

"At the Council, we entered on enquiries about improving the Plantations by silks, galls, flax, senna, etc., and considered how nutmegs and cinnamon might be obtained and brought to Jamaica, that soil and climate promising success. Dr. Worsley being called in, spake many considerable things to encourage it. We took order to send to the Plantations, that none of their ships should venture homeward single, but stay for company and convoys. We also deliberated on some fit person to go as Commissioner to inspect their actions in New England, and, from time to time, report how that people stood affected. — In future to meet at Whitehall." (Evelyn's Diary, II, p. 74.)

February 13.

Instructions from Secretary of State to prepare commission, etc., for New England Commissioners. (Cal., § 512.)

February 16.

Account of the militia in the Province of Maine read. (Cal., § 762.)

February 20.

Letter from Sir Thomas Lynch to the Council read. (Cal., § 640.)

March 1.

"A full Council of Plantations, on the danger of the Leeward Islands, threatened by the French, who had taken some of our ships, and began to interrupt our trade. Also in debate, whether the new governor of St. Christopher's should be subordinate to the Governor of Barbadoes. The debate was serious and long." (Evelyn's Diary, II, p. 75.)

April 2.

Report concerning the general state of the Leeward Is. and the differences depending between the English and French at St. Christopher. (Cal., § 850.)

April 9.

About Logwood (Journal; Cal., §§ 709, 742, 777, 825), and the defence of Barbadoes and the Leeward Is. (Cal., § 799.)

April 15.

Commission and instructions for Lord Willoughby and a report on his proposals. (Cal., § 850.)

April 16.

Letter from Sir Charles Wheeler read. (Cal., § 748.)

"Sat in Council, preparing Lord Willoughby's commission and instructions as governor of Barbadoes and the Caribbee Islands." (Evelyn's Diary, II, p. 78.)

April 19.

"At Council, preparing instructions for Colonel Stapleton, now to go Governor of St. Christopher's; and heard the complaints of the Jamaica merchants against the Spaniards, for hindering them from cutting logwood on the main land, where they have no pretence." (Evelyn's Diary, II, pp. 78–79.)

April 26.

Archibald Henderson's case. (Journal; Cal., §§ 775, p. 339, 806.)

April 30.

Commissioners for New England named, etc. (Journal; Cal., § 512.)

May 7.

Case of Mark Gabry, exporter of wool. (Cal., Dom., 1671–1672, pp. 155, 156, 481.)

May 10.

Case of the James of Belfast (Journal; Cal., § 813), and Wheeler letter (§ 775), containing a statement about Henderson.

Draft commission for Willoughby (§ 822).

Agreed that the commission for New England should be expedited (§ 512).

Report to the king upon the case of the William and Nicholas (§ 850).

May 14.

Proposals about the Leeward Is. formerly delivered by Lord Willoughby. (Journal; Cal., § 828.)

May 17.

Case of the William and Nicholas, Logwood ship. (Journal; Cal., §§ 823,

824.)

May 27.

Letter from Sir Thomas Lynch read. (Cal., § 777.)

June 4.

Consideration of the Logwood trade. (Journal; Cal., §§ 825, 837.)

June 11.

Order regarding ship William and Nicholas. (Cal., § 823.)

June 13.

Surinam and Curaçao. (Journal has "Quarasao"; Cal., § 879.)

June 15.

Continuation of the Logwood difficulty. (Journal; Cal., §§ 825, II, 879, 880.)

June 21.

Case of the Peter of London (Journal; Cal., § 820; Cal., Dom., 1673, pp. 198–199.)

Petition from Montserrat. (Journal; Cal., §§ 859, 879.)

June 25.

Jews in Jamaica. (Journal; Cal., §§ 848, 879.)

Heads of a letter to Sir Thomas Lynch from the Council. (Journal; Cal., § 943.)

Injuries from the French in the West Indies. (Journal; Cal., § 805.)

About ship departure from Jamaica. (Journal; Cal., §§ 683, 910.)

July 2.

Opinion and advice of the Council to the king upon a great variety of matters already discussed. Jews, logwood, Surinam, Jamaica defence, Curaçoa, Leeward Is. and Wheeler, and Stapleton, defense of Montserrat, etc. (Cal., § 879.) In addition the merchants seem to have made a report on the best time for ships to depart from Jamaica. (Journal.)

July 3.

Petition from the Long Islanders regarding the whale fishery and their relations with New Amsterdam read. (Cal., § 875.)

July 16.

Concerning Virginia—probably the question of the Arlington and Culpeper grant. (Journal.)

July 19.

Regarding the whale fishery. (Journal; Cal., § 875.)

July 26.

Petition of Sir Ernestus Biron, escheator in Barbadoes, read. (Journal; Cal., 1661–1668, § 1622.)

July 29.

Report on the petition. (Journal.)

September 1.

"Our Council of Plantations met at Lord Shaftesbury's (Chancellor of the Exchequer) to read and reform the draught of our new Patent, joining the Council of Trade to our political capacities." (Evelyn's Diary, II, p. 83.)

September 20.

Particulars of monies disbursed for the Council. (Journal.)

October 1 (about).

Letters written by Sir Thomas Lynch on June 20 and July 5 read to the Council. (Cal., § 943.)

COUNCIL FOR TRADE AND FOREIGN PLANTATIONS, 1672–1674.

October 13.

Commission opened and read and oath administered. (Journal.)

Letters from Gov. Stapleton and his answer to inquiries read. (Cal., §§ 842, 896.)

"Went to my Lord Keeper, (Sir Orlando Bridgeman) at Essex House, where our new patent was opened and read, constituting us that were of the Council of Plantations, to be now of the Council of Trade also, both united. After the patent was read, we all took our oaths, and departed." (Evelyn's Diary, II, p. 85.)

October 24.

Oaths administered. (Journal.)

"Met in Council, the Earl of Shaftesbury, now our President, swearing our Secretary and his clerks, which was Mr. Locke, an excellent learned gentleman, and student of Christ Church, Mr. Lloyd, and Mr. Frowde [son of Philip Frowde, clerk of the former Council of 1660]. We dispatched a letter to Sir Thomas Linch Governor of Jamaica, giving him notice of a design of the Dutch on that island." (Evelyn's Diary, II, p. 86.)

October 27.

Jamaica laws received and probably considered. (Cal., § 829.)

October 29.

Meeting held at 9. a. m. No statement as to business. (Cal., Dom., 1672–1673.)

November 3.

Logwood case; depositions and letters presented. (Cal., § 954.)

November 8.

New England case considered. (Journal.)

Letter from Sir Thomas Lynch read. (Cal., § 855.)

Rodney petition received from the Privy Council and read. (Cal., § 958.)

The petition from the consul of Venice, asking that consulage be levied on goods not on ships. (Journal; Cal., Dom., 1673, pp. 100, 303.)

"At Council we debated the business of the consulate of Leghorn (?). I was of the Committee with Sir Humphrey Winch, the Chairman, to examine the laws of his Majesty's several plantations and colonies in the West Indies, etc." (Evelyn's Diary, II, p. 86.)

November 13.

Letter from Dep. Gov. Coddrington of Barbadoes read. (Cal., §§ 872, 901, 902.)

November 15.

Petition of the consul at Venice considered further. (Journal.)

"Many merchants were summoned about the consulate of Venice; which caused great disputes; the most considerable thought it useless." (Evelyn's Diary, II, p. 86.)

November 20.

Petition of Rabba Couty, whose ship was seized at Port Royal, Jamaica, on the ground that he was a foreigner. (Cal., § 968; Cal., Dom., 1672–1673, p. 295.)

November 29.

Order of Council appointing a committee to confer with Sir Charles Wheeler. (Cal., § 974.)

December 7.

Report of the conferences. (Cal., § 977.)

December 10.

Report of the conferences. (Cal., § 977.)

December 20.

Report on the case of Rabba Couty, recommending the return of the vessel. (Cal., § 968, IV; Cal., Dom., 1672–1673, p. 295.)

Order issued for a more speedy and orderly despatch of reports to the King and of letters and orders to the Governors of plantations. (Cal., Dom., 1672–1673, p. 295.)

December 21.

"Settled the Consulate of Venice." (Evelyn's Diary. II, p. 86.)

December 29.

Report on petition of the Gambia merchants regarding the use of a wood called "sanders" for dyeing purposes. (Cal., § 973, III; Cal., Dom., 1673, pp. 190, 217.)

1673.

January 7.

Letter of Sir Thomas Lynch; complaint of Gambia Company; Russell's answer to Rodney's petition; report on laws of Jamaica; articles relating to the Venetian trade; Ordinance in Sweden against "our privileges"; St. Christopher business; answer to Col. Stapleton; advice to the King about planting St. Christopher; regarding the books and papers of the former councils; Newfoundland trade; acts of Barbadoes. (Cal., Dom., 1672–1673, p. 403. This series of subjects is the only complete list of the heads of a single day's business that we find anywhere, except in the minutes of two meetings noted below.)

January 9.

About Johnson "the Pyrat." (Cal., §§ 938, 1082, Index; Journal.)

January 11.

Order of the Council to the secretary to report on losses and injuries lately sustained from the Spaniards. (Cal., § 1022.)

February 1.

Similar order regarding the differences with the French at St. Christopher. (Cal., §§ 1028, 1033.)

Heads of a letter to Gov. Stapleton of St. Christopher. (Journal.)

February 6.

Gambia Adventurers. (Journal.)

February 18.

> Gambia Adventurers. (Journal.)

> Secretary's report on St. Christopher. (Cal., § 1034.) Secretary ordered to prepare another report for the 25th on same subject.

February 25.

> Secretary's report probably presented on this day.

March 6.

> Letter to Gov. Stapleton written. (Journal.)

> Letter from Lord Willoughby read. (Cal., § 1000.)

March 17.

> Petition from Rodney asking that a certain Carpenter, "who has long lived in Nevis," may be heard. (Cal., § 1049.)

> Reply of Capt Rodney to the answer of Gov. Russell read. (Cal., § 1050.)

April 10.

> Heads of an address about St. Christopher. (Journal; Cal., §§ 1038, 1069.)

> New England. (Journal.)

April 14.

> Representations on Gambia question drawn up. (Cal., Dom., 1773, p. 142.)

April 22.

> Rodney's petition. (Journal; Cal., §§ 958, 1049–1050, 1071, 1074, 1110, 1194, 1225. See Index.)

June 9.

> Address of Council to the king regarding differences between the English and the French at St. Christopher. (Cal., §§ 903, 1105.)

June 23.

> Representation and advice of the Council regarding the Rodney case. (Cal., § 1110.)

> "To London, to accompany our Council, who went in a body to congratulate the new Lord Treasurer [Sir Thomas Osborne], no friend to it, because promoted by my Lord Arlington, whom he hated." (Evelyn's Diary, II, p. 90.)

July 21.

> About the exportation of wool (Journal); report on this question urging

that present laws be put in execution and export of wool be strictly forbidden. (Cal., Dom., 1673, pp. 382, 541.)

September 13.

Dr Worsley, his discharge. (Journal; Cal., § 1151.)

September 16.

To Council about chosing a new Secretary. (Evelyn's Diary, II, p. 94.)

October 15.

Mr. Lock sworne. (Journal; Cal., §§ 1162, 1163.)

"To Council, and swore in Mr. Locke, secretary, Dr. Worsley being dead." (Evelyn's Diary, II, 95. This statement regarding Dr. Worsley cannot be true.)

October 21 (committee).

Charter parties for transporting to Barbadoes stores and provisions read. (Cal., § 1058.)

Letters from Sir Peter Colleton & others read. (Cal., §§ 1101, 1104, 1131, 1133.)

Regarding capture of New York. (Cal., §§ 1138, 1157.)

October 27 (committee).

About Sir J. Atkins, Barbadoes. (Journal.)

Regarding New York; Mr. Dyer's project for reducing that town. (Journal; Cal., § 1157.)

"To Council about sending succours to recover New York; and then we read the commission and instructions to Sir Jonathan Atkins, the new Governor of Barbadoes." (Evelyn's Diary, II, 95.)

November 3.

About New York, Albany, etc.; consideration of the retaking of these places from the Dutch. (Journal; Cal., §§ 1160, 1165.)

November 7 (committee).

William Dervell's statement regarding the loss of New York. (Cal., § 1143.)

November 8.

Barbadoes and Sir J. Atkins. (Journal.) Probably the question of Atkins's commission as Governor of Barbadoes was here under consideration.

November 19 (committee).

Letters from Gov. Lynch read. (Cal., § 1115.)

November 24.

Petitions of Steed, provost marshal of Barbadoes, read. (Cal., § 1167.)

December 1.

Letter from Sir Jonathan Atkins received and (probably) read. (Cal., § 1173.)

December 5.

Deposition of William Carpenter in favor of Steed. (Cal., § 1177.)

December 19.

Report to the King, presenting draft of commission and instructions for Sir Jonathan Atkins, governor of Barbadoes. (Cal., §§ 1182, 1185.)

1674.

January 7.

Received order from Privy Council committee on grievances regarding the Rodney petition. (Cal., § 1194.)

January 10 (committee).

Petition of William Dyer of New York to the King read. (Cal., § 1108.)

January 16.

Report of the Council on this petition. (Cal., § 1108.)

January 23.

Order from the Privy Council instructing the Council to transmit a true state of the case between Rodney and others. (Cal., § 1207.)

February 10.

"Ordered, That a Copy of Mr. Rodneys Petičon and his Maties. Reference thereupon, and the Report of this Councill should bee delivered by Mr. Lock to Mr. Secretry. Coventry to bee by him pesented to his Maty.

The Earle of Arlingtons Lr̃e to this Councill of the 23d. of January last signifying his M̃aties. pleasure, That this Councill should consider of a Comn. & Inſtruc̃cons for the Earle of Carlisle, appointed to bee Governor. of Jamaica, and Col: Morgan appointed to bee Deputy Governor. was read.

A Draught of Inſtruc̃cons for my Lord Carlisle was read and debated, and the further debate thereof adjourned till next meeting.

My Lord Culpeper having acquainted this Councill, that my Lord Carlisle had something to offer to this Councill. The Councill desired my Lord Culpeper to acquaint his Lordsp, That if hee pleased to come to the Councill on Fryday next in the Afternoone, they shall bee ready to receive what ev his Lordsp shall bee pleas'd to offer to them.

Ordered that Mr. Lock gett some Presses made wherein the papers belong to this Councill may bee conveniently layd up.

Two Addiconall Inſtruccõns for Sr. Jonathan Atkins Ordered to bee drawne, one to pevent his making of Judges & Justices by Comns. limited in tyme, becaus some former Governors. by cõmissionating these Officers only for a yeare, kept them at their devoçõn for feare they should bee left out of the next, thereby eluding their Inſtruccõns, which forbid the turning out of any of these Officers, but for good caus. Another to prevent the perpetuity of Laws in the Plantaçõns wthout his Maties confirmaçõn. Ordered also that the Addres to his Maty abt. Jonathan Atkins and others Governors. taking the Oath's here, to be drawne wthout Preamble." (Shaftesbury Papers, Div. X, 8 (8).)

February 17.

"Mr. Locke Reported to the Councill, That attending Mr. Secretary Coventry wth the papers concerning Rodney's Case ordered by this Council the 10th of this Instant February, Mr. Secretary Coventry told him, That the Order of the Privy Councill being to transmitt the said papers, to his Maty in Councill, that itt was not proper to do itt by his hands, Butt that they should bee sent to one of the Clerks of the Councill to bee by him delivered.

Ordered thereupon, That the said papers bee delivered to one of the Clerks of the Councill, to bee by him pesented to his Maty in Councill.

Ordered That the Address of this Councill to his Maty concerning Sr. Jonathan Atkins and other Governors. and Deputy Governors. takeing the Oathes &c: here, bee delivered to the Earle of Arlington to bee by him pesented to his Maty.

Two Addiconall Inſtruccõns for Sr. Jonathan Atkins, The one about the Comns. of Justices of the Peace, and the other about Marshall Law read & agreed.

A Copy of an Order of the Presidts. & Councill of Barbados, concerning the Provost Marshall's place, was brought in by my Lord Culpeper, who assured the Councill hee had reçed itt in a Letter from the Clerk of the Councill there, which letter hee had not now about him. The consideraçõn thereof adjourned till this Copy bee made appeare to this Councill to bee more authentique.

Upon Reading the Addiconall Inſtruccõn to Sir Jonathan Atkins concerning the reenacting of Laws. The Councill entred into a debate about the best way for his Maty to confirme the Laws made by the Plantaçõns, which being often tymes ill worded by the Assembly there, and some tymes faulty in some part though the maine deserves to bee established. Which being found to bee a matter of great moment, The farther debate thereof was adjourned till another opportunity, when the Earle of Shaftesbury should bee present." (Shaftesbury Papers, Div. X, 8 (9); Cal., § 1221. These minutes are the only complete record that we have of the proceedings at council meetings. They show how much has been lost in the disappearance of the original journal.)

March 6.

Letter from Lord Willoughby read. (Cal., § 966.)

Petition of William Helyar regarding woodland purchased by him in Jamaica. (Cal., § 1236.)

March 8.

Report of the Council upon the petition of Edwin Steed. (Cal., § 1238.)

March 17.

Mr. Gorges paper regarding the sugar plantations. (Cal., § 1244.)

March 23.

Sends Helyar's petition to Gov. Lynch and wishes reply. (Cal., § 1250.)

Draft Commission for the Earl of Carlisle, appointed governor of Jamaica. (Cal., §§ 1251, 1252. Cf. § 1253.)

Similar draft for Col. Morgan, deputy governor of Jamaica. (Cal., § 1254.)

April 3.

Petition from Representatives of Leeward Is. for convoys, etc. (Cal., § 1257.)

April 13.

New England: petition of Earl of Sterling, Gorges, and Mason read. (Journal; Cal., § 1247.)

May 8 (committee).

Letter from Gov. Stapleton read. (Cal., §§ 1201–1203, 1327.)

July 3.

Petition of Edmund Cooke, merchant, regarding the barbarous treatment received from the Spaniards. (Cal., § 1320.)

July 17.

Similar petition from other merchants. (Cal., § 1327.)

September 15.

"To Council, about fetching away the English left at Surinam, etc., since our reconciliation with Holland." (Evelyn's Diary, II, p. 99.)

September 22.

Regarding Surinam question—fetching the English away, etc. (Cal., § 1354.)

September 24.

Report on this question to the King. (Cal., § 1355.)

October 6 (Committee).

Letter from Gov. Lynch in answer to Col. Helyar's petition read. (Cal., § 1301.)

October 13.

Letter from Gov. Stapleton on the wrongs suffered from the French in the Leeward Is. (Cal., § 1333.)

October 15.

Proposal read of F. Gorges, agent of Gov. Stapleton, regarding the action of the French. (Cal., § 1360.)

October 16.

St. Christopher and Sir William Lockhart's letter. (Cal., § 1365, I.) Lockhart was "Resident with the French King."

October 27.

Discussion of the Surinam situation. (Journal.)

October 30.

Continuation of the same. (Journal.)

November 17.

Continuation of the same. (Journal.)

"To Council, on the business of Surinam, where the Dutch had detained some English in prison, ever since the first war, 1665." (Evelyn's Diary, II, 100.)

November 20.

About Negroes; probably regarding a clause in Lord Vaughan's commission. (Journal; Cal., §§ 1386, 1392.)

November 21.

Jamaica and my Lord Vaughan. (Journal.)

November 24.

Heads of Lord Vaughan's commission and instructions. (Cal., § 1392). About Negroes. (Journal.)

December 4.

About Surinam. Address of the Council to the King (Journal; Cal., § 1401.)

December 17.

Address of the Council regarding Indians brought by force from Guinea to Barbadoes. (Cal., § 1409.)

December 18.

About Surinam. (Journal.) Instruction for a vessel sailing to that island. (Cal., §§ 1413, 1414, 1415.)

December 22.

Address from the Council to the King regarding the Surinam question. (Cal., § 1416.)

Lector House believes that a society develops through a two-fold approach of continuous learning and adaptation, which is derived from the study of classic literary works spread across the historic timeline of literature records. Therefore, we aim at reviving, repairing and redeveloping all those inaccessible or damaged but historically as well as culturally important literature across subjects so that the future generations may have an opportunity to study and learn from past works to embark upon a journey of creating a better future.

This book is a result of an effort made by Lector House towards making a contribution to the preservation and repair of original ancient works which might hold historical significance to the approach of continuous learning across subjects.

HAPPY READING & LEARNING!

LECTOR HOUSE LLP
E-MAIL: lectorpublishing@gmail.com

9 789356 140172

Ingram Content Group UK Ltd.
Milton Keynes UK
UKHW012243150323
418612UK00003B/142